The Infall…
of the
Prophets

عليهم السلام

The Infallibility of the Prophets

عليهم السلام

عِصمَةُ الأنبِيَاءِ عليهم السلام

Imam & Exegete
Muhammad ʿAlī al-Ṣābūnī

Foreword by
Muhammad b. Yahya b. Muhammad al-Ninowy

Translated & Annotated by
Rayshaud Jameer

BEACON BOOKS

First published in the UK by Beacon Books and Media Ltd
Innospace, Chester Street, Manchester M1 5GD, UK.

First paperback edition published 2018
Printed in the UK
www.beaconbooks.net

Cataloging-in-Publication record for this book is available from the British Library

ISBN Paperback 978-0-9926335-6-1

Cover concept by OUTSTANDING standoutnow.co.uk
Cover design by Bipin Mistry

Contents

Preface vii

Introduction 1

1. The Infallibility of the Prophets ﷺ 17

   The Definition of Infallibility 17

   Allah's Protection for His Prophet Muhammad ﷺ since Childhood 20

2. Does Infallibility Apply before or after Prophethood? 23

   Does Infallibility apply to Non-Prophets? 26

   The Belief of the People of the Book about the Prophets ﷺ 28

3. Seemingly Unclear Matters about the Infallibility of Prophets ﷺ and their Invalidating Responses 33

4. The Ostensible Disobedience of Prophet Adam ﷺ 35

5. The Infallibility of Prophet Ibrahim ﷺ 41

   What were the Three 'Lies' (equivocations) of Ibrahim ﷺ? 48

6. The Infallibility of Prophet Yusuf ﷺ 51

   Fabrication and Slander 51

   The Incorrect Interpretation 53

   The Correct Interpretation 53

   Ten Proofs for the Infallibility of Yusuf ﷺ 56

7. The Infallibility of Prophet Nuh ﷺ 63

8. The Infallibility of Prophet Yunus ﷺ 65

   The Incorrect Interpretation 65

   The Correct Interpretation 65

9. Was the Messenger of Allah ﷺ made to make Mistakes? 69

   Ten Verses about the 'Censure' of the Messenger of Allah ﷺ and their Correct Interpretations 69

   The First Verse 70

      The First Narration 71

The Second Narration ... 72
The Second Verse ... 75
The Third Verse ... 78
The Fourth Verse ... 80
The Fifth Verse ... 81
The Sixth Verse ... 83
The Seventh Verse ... 85
The Eighth Verse ... 87
The Ninth Verse ... 89
The Tenth Verse ... 91

Appendix: Two False Attributions to Prophet Dawud ﷺ ... 97
Index of Quranic Verses ... 101
Index of Hadith ... 117

Preface

Muslims have always had an inherent sense of what is sacred because of the deep reverence they hold for their Prophet ﷺ and his wont (*Sunna*). Whether in mundane habits like beginning actions from the right side, pronouncing the Name of God before eating, or opening one's home to strangers, Muslims all over the globe cling firmly and dearly to the past traditions of the Prophet ﷺ and the saints of the golden generation—his Companions ﷺ.

Even today in the 'modern world', we see Islam being the last of the Abrahamic religions to hold fast to the ancient aniconism found in the teachings of Prophets Moses, Jesus and Muhammad ﷺ.

Aniconism is the practice of or belief in the shunning of images of beings, Prophets or other respected religious figures, or any human beings or living creatures. The term aniconic may be used to describe the absence of graphic representations in a particular belief system, regardless of whether an injunction against them exists or not.

It is plain for anyone with a spiritual eye that has not been blighted to see that sanctity is slowly being eroded by the spiritually-blinded monoculture in which we live. Whether it is the Charlie Hebdo or Danish cartoon incidents, the judge in New Mexico who decreed that the Ten Commandments should be removed in front of a courthouse at the behest of two Wiccans citing promotion of religious beliefs, or Larry David's urinating on the picture of Prophet Jesus ﷺ, there is a disturbingly growing trend attempting to eliminate the inviolability of the Messengers of God.

Professor Timothy Winter states in a recent publication:

"...Charlie Hebdo, like the Danish magazine Jyllands-Posten several years ago,[1] *did*

[1] This refers to the infamous Danish cartoons incident that depicted deriding and insulting cartoons of the Prophet Muhammad ﷺ. The cartoons attempting to lampoon Prophet Muhammad ﷺ began after the Danish newspaper Jyllands-Posten published 12 editorial cartoons on 30 September 2005, most of which depicted Prophet Muhammad ﷺ in derogatory scenes. The newspaper announced that this was an attempt to contribute to the debate about criti-

not simply publish images of the Prophet. That, on its own, would probably have occasioned little comment. The difficulty lay in the evident intention to mock, deride and wound. To portray the Prophet naked, or with a bomb in his turban, was not the simple manufacturing of a graven image. It was received, and rightly so, as a deliberate insult to an already maligned and vulnerable community."

Infallibility in Other Traditions

The doctrine in the Roman Catholic Church refers to the concept that in specific circumstances, the Pope is incapable of error in issuing papal decrees, in other words, infallible. In Shi'a theology, the *Ahl al-Bayt* or the Family of the Prophet ﷺ and the Twelve Shi'a Imams are all infallible and do not make mistakes in the sense that all of their teachings can be relied upon to be certainly true and that they have complete knowledge about right and wrong and never intend to disobey God.

While these two traditions both relegate the notion of infallibility to non-prophets, the way of orthodox Sunni Islam (*Ahl al-Sunna wa al-Jama'*) has drawn a very clear line in the sand stating that the Prophets, and only the Prophets عليهم السلام, are infallible to the exclusion of all else.

The Understanding of Infallibility Amongst Muslims

In the Muslim Community, the Prophets and Messengers عليهم السلام are held in the highest regard as the pinnacle of God's creation—the best of the best and sinless.

Unfortunately, within the Muslim Community there are misunderstandings regarding the Prophets. Whether it be the famous movie about Islam entitled *The Message* or the self-titled television series which aired in 2012 about the life of our master ʿUmar b. al-Khattāb رضي الله عنه to name a few examples, many Muslims are not quite sure about how to approach the religiously-sensitive issue of depicting religious figures, particularly the Prophets عليهم السلام.

In the Western world, seemingly innocent speakers, sermonizers, and 'edu-tainers,' have been known to throw out deprecating statements about various Prophets and their so-called 'sins' without batting

---

cism of Islam and self-censorship. Muslim groups in Denmark were in uproar, complained, and the incident eventually led to protests around the world, including demonstrations and riots in some Muslim countries.

an eye. For students of the Islam's Sacred Knowledge, this can feel like a slap on the ear.

In this detailed yet succinct treatise, an academic giant of our time, Imam al-Ṣābunī (may Allah preserve him) skillfully dispels any aspersions or misunderstandings from the life and times of the Noble Prophets and Messengers of God (upon them all be peace).

Biography of Imam Ṣābunī

He is Muhammad Ali al-Ṣābunī, one of the leading scholars of Sunni orthodox Islam (Ahl al-Sunna wa al-Jama') in the current era. A specialist in the knowledge of the Holy Quran's exegesis, he has authored one of the best and most widely accepted exegesis (tafsir) of the Quran in this era entitled Ṣafwat al-Tafāsīr (The Choicest Selections from the Books of Exegesis).

Background

Born in the city of Aleppo, Syria in 1930 CE, his studies began early in his life at the hands of his father Shaykh Jamil al-Ṣābunī, who was one of the senior scholars in Aleppo city in his own right. He began *ḥifẓ* or memorizing the Quran in a *madrasa* or seminary and completed his *ḥifẓ* in secondary school. He learnt the ancillary disciplines of the Arabic language, knowledge of inheritance and the other sciences of Islam from Shaykh Muhammad Najīb Sirāj, Ahmad al-Shamāʿ, Muhammad Saʿīd, and other scholars.

His Studies

He began his studies in the city of Aleppo at a School of Business where he studied for one year before becoming averse because of its teaching students about interest-based transactions. Despite obtaining excellent results, he left to pursue studies in the disciplines of the Sharia at the famed Khaswarīyya School of Sharia in Aleppo and graduated in 1949. Thereafter, the Syrian Ministry of Endowments sponsored him to study at Masjid al-Azhar in Cairo and he graduated from the Faculty of Sharia in 1952, completed his specialization and further obtained a degree in Sharia Rulings (*Qaḍā*) in 1954.

His Academic Life

After completing his studies at al-Azhar, he returned to Syria to work as a professor in the Ministry of Islamic Culture in Aleppo and he continued teaching there until 1962. Subsequently, he relocated to the Kingdom of Saudi Arabia to work as a lecturer on behalf of the Syrian Ministry of *Tarbiya* and Education for the Sharia College of Islamic Teachings and the *Tarbiya* College at *Umm al-Qura'* University in Mecca al-Mukarrama and was tenured there for approximately thirty years. Following that, he worked as an academic researcher in the Centre for Academic Research and Reviving the Islamic Heritage. Thereafter, he worked in the Muslim World League as a counsellor for scientific research in the Quran and Sunna, and remained there for a number of years.

The Shaykh has a voluminous and acute aptitude for knowledge. He had a daily class in Masjid al-Haram in Mecca al-Mukarrama in which he would issue edicts (*fatwa*). Simultaneously, he also held a weekly class in one of the mosques in the city of Jeddah which ran for approximately eight years in which he explained to students of knowledge more than one-third of the Holy Quran. These lessons were recorded on audio cassettes. In a similar fashion, the Shaykh has over 600 complete *tafsir* of Quran programs recorded for television. This production for this project took over two years to complete and was completed in the year 1998 CE.

A Selection of his Works

1. *Ṣafwat al-tafāsīr* ("The Choicest of Exegesis") - his most famous book which combines two different types of exegesis, namely *tafsir ma'thūr* and *manqūl* extracted from the foremost *tafsirs*, namely *Ṭabarī*, *Kashshāf*, *Qurṭubī*, *'Ālūsī*, *Ibn Kathīr*, *Baḥr Muḥīt*, and others in a simplified presentation.
2. *Al-Mawārīth fi al-shari'a al-islāmī* ("Inheritance in Islamic Law")
3. *Rawā'i' al-bayān fi tafsir āyāt al-aḥkām* ("Enjoyable Elucidations Explaining the Verses of Quran")
4. *Qabs min nīr al-Qurān al-Karīm* ("A Firebrand of Light from the Holy Quran")
5. *Al-Sunna al-nabawīyya qasm min al-waḥy al-ilāhī al-munazzal* ("The Prophetic Sunna: A Portion of Divine Revelation")

6. *Mawsūʿa al-fiqh al-shariʿ al-muyassar* ("A Simplified Encyclopedia of Islamic Jurisprudence")
7. *Al-Ziwāj al-islāmī al-mubakkir: saʿāda wa hiṣāna* ("An Early Islamic Marriage: Felicity and Chastity")
8. *Tafsir al-wāḍiḥ al-muyassir* ("The Simplified and Clear Tafsir")
9. *Al-Mahdi al-nabawī al-ṣaḥīḥ fi salāh al-tarāwīh* ("Correct Prophetic Guidance regarding Tarāwīh Prayers")
10. *Al-Nabūwwa wa al-anbiyā'* ("Prophethood and the Prophets")
11. *Mawqif al-shariʿa al-gharra' min nikāḥ al-mut'āh* ("The Resplendent Sharia's Stance on Temporary Marriage")
12. *Al-Mahdi wa ashrāt al-saʿāh* ("The Mahdi and the Portents of the Hour")
13. *Sharḥ riyāḍ al-ṣāliḥīn* ("Commentary on the Meadows of the Righteous")
14. *Shubuhāt wa abāṭīl ḥawl taʿaddud zawjāt al-rasūl* ("Abstrusities and Calumnies around the Polygyny of the Prophet s")
15. *Tibyān fi 'ulūm al-Qurān* ("The Elucidation on the Sciences of the Quran")
16. *Risalah fi ḥukm taṣwīr* ("The Treatise on the Ruling of Photography")
17. *Jarīmah al-ribā akhtār al-jarā'im al-dīnīyya wa al-ijtimā'īyya* ("The Crime of Usury is the Most Dangerous of Religious and Societal Crimes")

At the time of this writing, the Shaykh is in good health and spirits, living in Mecca al-Mukarrama; may Allah continue to shade us by him. *Amin.*

Introduction

By Shaykh Muhammad b. Yahya al-Ninowy

All praise belongs to Allah, Lord of the Worlds. May peace and blessings be upon His Noble Prophets Whom He sent as bearers of glad-tidings and warners, and as mercies from Him to the worlds. He selected them from the noblest of lineages in His creation, He safeguarded them, protected them, chose them for Himself, supported them with His Revelations, revealed to them His Books, sent to them His Angels, and tasked them with that which he did not task any other. Accordingly, He aided them in their duties and granted them unparalleled distinctions and adorned them with the loftiest qualities. So may Allah send peace and blessings upon them in this life and in the everlasting life.

To proceed: Ustadh Rashad Jameer (Allah preserve him and protect him) requested me to write an introduction for *The Infallibility of the Prophets* ﷺ authored by the ʿAllamah, the Shaykh, Imam al-Sabuni (Allah preserve him), so I obliged him in that despite being unworthy, in hopes of being included among all those who defend the Noble Prophets; may Allah unite us and them in the Kingdom of Heaven. *Amin!*

From the onset, it behooves us to delve into the linguistic meaning of the Arabic word *ʿiṣmah* or infallibility, as well as its meaning when used as a technical term in Islamic nomenclature. Thereafter we will offer concise proofs for it, then conclude by mentioning some of the most important books authored on this topic. So seeking the aid of Almighty Allah, I declare:

The Linguistic Meaning of ʿIṣmah

Linguistically, *ʿismah* or infallibility means 'to prevent.' It is said that the root meaning of *ʿismah* is 'to fasten' or 'to bind,' then later it took on the meaning 'to prevent.' Also, *ʿismah* means protection (*hifz*), and Allah's protection for his servant means that He protects him from his destruction i.e. He safeguards and preserves him. Allah says:

وَنَادَىٰ نُوحٌ ابْنَهُ وَكَانَ فِي مَعْزِلٍ يَا بُنَيَّ ارْكَب مَّعَنَا وَلَا تَكُن مَّعَ الْكَافِرِينَ
قَالَ سَآوِي إِلَىٰ جَبَلٍ **يَعْصِمُنِي** مِنَ الْمَاءِ ۚ قَالَ لَا **عَاصِمَ** الْيَوْمَ مِنْ أَمْرِ اللَّهِ إِلَّا مَن
رَّحِمَ ۚ وَحَالَ بَيْنَهُمَا الْمَوْجُ فَكَانَ مِنَ الْمُغْرَقِينَ

﴾*And it sailed with them through waves like mountains, and Noah called to his son who was apart [from them], "O my son, come aboard with us and be not with the disbelievers." [But] he said, "I will take refuge on a mountain* ***to protect me*** *from the water." [Noah] said, "There is no* ***protector*** *today from the decree of Allah, except for whom He gives mercy." And the waves came between them, and he was among the drowned.*﴿ [Surah Hud:42-43]

Allah's saying: ﴾*...I will take refuge on a mountain to protect me from the water...*﴿ means it will protect me (*ya'simuni*) from drowning. And Allah's saying: ﴾*There is no protector today...*﴿ means there is no protector nor defender today (*la 'āsim al-yawm*).

Allah says:

قَالَتْ فَذَٰلِكُنَّ الَّذِي لُمْتُنَّنِي فِيهِ ۖ وَلَقَدْ رَاوَدتُّهُ عَن نَّفْسِهِ **فَاسْتَعْصَمَ** ۖ وَلَئِن لَّمْ يَفْعَلْ
مَا آمُرُهُ لَيُسْجَنَنَّ وَلَيَكُونًا مِّنَ الصَّاغِرِينَ

﴾*She said, "That is the one about whom you blamed me. And I certainly sought to seduce him,* ***but he firmly refused;*** *and if he will not do what I order him, he will surely be imprisoned and will be of those debased."*﴿
[Surah Yusuf:32]

The meaning of ﴾*...but he firmly refused...*﴿ (*ist'asam*) is that he sought protection and refuge (*iltaja'a*).

As for it being interpreted to mean that he attempted to protect himself, or that he attempted to save her from her distress and went to her— which is among the technical usages of the word *'ismah*—then this is not the intended meaning of the word here. That particular meaning was merely adopted later on because of the near-synonymous meanings of 'seeking refuge' and 'seeking protection.' And the two meanings are both correct in the sense of 'seeking refuge *in Allah*,' as Allah says:

قُلْ مَن ذَا الَّذِي **يَعْصِمُكُم مِّنَ اللَّهِ** إِنْ أَرَادَ بِكُمْ سُوءًا أَوْ أَرَادَ بِكُمْ رَحْمَةً ۚ
وَلَا يَجِدُونَ لَهُم مِّن دُونِ اللَّهِ وَلِيًّا وَلَا نَصِيرًا

﴾*Say, "Who is it that can* ***protect you from Allah*** *if He intends for you an ill or intends for you a mercy?" And they will not find for themselves besides Allah any protector or any helper.*﴿
[Surah Ahzab:17]

And Allah says:

وَكَيْفَ تَكْفُرُونَ وَأَنتُمْ تُتْلَىٰ عَلَيْكُمْ آيَاتُ اللَّهِ وَفِيكُمْ رَسُولُهُ ۗ وَمَن **يَعْتَصِم بِاللَّهِ** فَقَدْ هُدِيَ إِلَىٰ صِرَاطٍ مُّسْتَقِيمٍ

﴿*And how could you disbelieve while to you are being recited the verses of Allah and among you is His Messenger? And whoever* ***holds firmly to Allah*** *has [indeed] been guided to a straight path.*﴾

[*Surah Al-ʿImran:101*]

Ibn Mandhur states in *Lisan al-ʿArab* under the letters عصم:

> In the language of the Arabs, *ʿismah* refers to prevention (*manaʿa*) and protection, and Allah's protection for His servant refers to His protecting him from perdition. As Allah says in the Quran: ﴿*"There is no protector today from the decree of Allah, except for whom He gives mercy."*﴾ Someone seeks protection from Allah when he seeks Allah's help to avert and prevent harm from him. *ʿIsmah* also refers to *hifz* or safeguarding.
>
> The word is used in a sentence saying: "The food *ʿasamahu* or protected him," i.e. it staved off hunger from him. The form of the word *istaʿsama* was used in the Quran when the Minister's wife attempted to seduce Prophet Yusuf (upon him be peace) but he *istaʿsama* or downright refused, i.e. he actively refused and did not accept her immoral proposal.

The Technical Meaning of ʿIṣmah

Regarding the technical meaning of *ʿiṣmah,* a definitive text containing the word *ʿiṣmah* has not been transmitted in the Quran and Sunnah. Instead, it is the scholars that have coined this technical term and applied it to the Noble Prophets (upon them be peace) to refer to the meanings of Allah's selecting them, protecting them, preventing them from sin, and safeguarding them from lapses. The scholars are in agreement about the fundamental principle of this technical term and disagree about its details and finer points. The fundamental principle in which all agree is that: The infallibility of the Noble Prophets (upon them be peace) means that Allah selected them to be His Noble Messengers to His creation and the means (*wasila*) for His Revelation. With great care, He chose them, cast upon them Divine Love from Himself, and bestowed unto them such unique and special distinctions (*khasa'is*) that He did not give to anyone else in creation. He connected them to

Him and protected them at all times, and safeguarded them from disbelief, major sins, and foul and vile minor sins—both before receiving Prophethood and after it. He preserved them regarding their conveying the correct, complete, and perfect Message of Islam without any deficiency, remissness, or forgetfulness.

Given that a complete and explicit definition of *ʿiṣmah* is not expressly stated in the Quran, the scholars endeavoured to compile relevant Quranic verses on this topic, such as Imam Fakhr al-Din al-Razi in his book entitled *ʿIsmah al-anbiya*. This, despite the fact that the core concept of infallibility that was understood by all scholars is found entirely in the Quran and spread throughout its radiant verses. Its proofs are implicit, not explicit, as is the case with the Sunnah.

And since the terminology *ʿismah* or infallibility as we understand it today is not expressly mentioned in the Quran, nor in the Sunnah, nor has it been transmitted from the Companions, nor the Followers (*Tabiʿīn*), then without doubt, it is a novel term that has its origins after the Golden Era of Prophecy.

Scholars Deduced the Concept of Infallibility from Definitive Sacred Texts and Reason

The reason and objective behind Allah's sending the Noble Prophets (upon them be peace) was to guide humanity to the straight path which leads to eternal success in this world, and the good-pleasure of the Lord of the Worlds in the hereafter. But how could they have guided humanity down a path which they knew not, or which they contradicted in their words, deeds, or states?! Moreover, just as the Noble Prophets (upon them be peace) are tasked with conveying the revelation and the Message of Allah to people and guiding them to the straight path, likewise, they are tasked to purify the souls of people (*tazkiya*), to gradually nurture them (*tarbiya*), rectify them (*islah*), and to take individuals who are both ready and willing to the highest stages of human perfection. Accordingly, it is imperative that they themselves be at the peak of perfection in knowledge, in teaching, in the ability to gradually develop others (*tarbiya*), in offering guidance, understanding, purification, and other attributes. And just as they guide people to that which increases their proximity to Allah Most High and their connection to Him and awareness of Him, then so too must they themselves always be upon the highest levels of connection and closeness to Allah Most High.

The Rational Proofs for the Infallibility of the Prophets

1. The Quran describes some individuals as ***mukhlas*** or chosen, referring to those whom Allah chose for *khulās* (salvation) and *ikhlāṣ* (sincerity) such that no one is able to misguide them—not even the devil himself, as the Quran states:

> ﴾*[Iblīs] said, "By your might, I will surely mislead them all, except, among them, Your chosen servants (mukhlaṣīn)."*﴿
>
> [Surah Sad:42-43]

And Allah says:

> ﴾*And [mention] when We said to the angels, "Prostrate to Adam," and they prostrated, except for Iblis. He said, "Should I prostrate to one You created from clay?" [Iblīs] said, "Do You see this one whom You have honoured above me? If You grant me respite until the Day of Resurrection, I will surely destroy his descendants, except for a few." [Allah] said, "Go, for whoever of them follows you, indeed Hell will be the recompense of you all - an ample recompense. And incite [to senselessness] whoever you can among them with your voice and assault them with your horses and foot soldiers and become a partner in their wealth and their children and promise them." But Satan does not promise them except delusion. Indeed, over My [believing] servants there is for you no authority. And sufficient is your Lord as Disposer of affairs.*﴿
>
> [Isra:61-64]

Undeniably, the Noble Prophets (upon them be peace) are protected by the Power and Authority of Allah from the misguiding devils. So although these verses do not contain an explicit proof that specifically targets the Noble Prophets (upon them be peace), however, the Noble Prophets (upon them be peace) are certainly protected by the Power and Authority of Allah from misguiding devils because it is inconceivable and illogical to presume that these verses do not apply to them.

The Quran has also conferred some of the Noble Prophets (upon them be peace) with the honorific title of *mukhlasīn*, as the Quran states:

> ﴾*And remember Our servants Ibrahim and Ishaq and Yaqoub, men of power and insight. Surely We purified them by a pure quality, remembrance of the (final) abode [in the hereafter].*﴿
>
> [Surah Sad:45-46]

Allah also says:

﴾*And mention Musa in the Book; surely he was one purified, and he was a messenger, a prophet.*﴿

[Surah Maryam:51]

Likewise, the reason why Prophet Yusuf (upon him be peace) was exonerated from all charges and removed from those intensely dark times was because he was *mukhlas*, as Allah states:

﴾*And she certainly determined to seduce him, and he would have inclined to her had he not seen the proof of his Lord. And thus [it was that We averted from him evil and immorality. Indeed, he was of Our chosen servants (mukhlasīn).*﴿

[*Surah* Yusuf:24]

2. The Quran commands all mankind—without exception—to obey the Noble Prophets, as Allah states:

﴾*And We did not send any messenger except to be obeyed by permission of Allah...*﴿

[*Surah* Nisa:64]

And Allah states:

﴾*Say, "Obey Allah and the Messenger." But if they turn away - then indeed, Allah does not like the disbelievers.*﴿

[Al-'Imran:32]

Now, unconditional obedience to them is in regards to what is in accordance to the obedience of Allah in all aspects, such that obeying them should never contradict and oppose the obedience of Allah—not in anything major nor minor, not at the current time nor in the future. Otherwise, the command for unconditional obedience would be for Allah alone. As for a command to adhere to unconditional obedience to those who are susceptible to sins and deviance—even in one issue or a trivial matter—then in reality, this is a command to follow that sin, or is folly, or there is a lack of wisdom in the command, and Allah utterly transcends beyond such things.

Now when it comes to our Prophet (Allah bless and give peace to him and his family), Allah clearly declares the supreme piety and godliness the Noble Prophet possessed in every aspect of his life, the perfection of his connection with His Lord in every way, and his mute tongue of eloquence (or demeanour) was speaking about his Lord in every way, his state with his Lord in everything he did, as Allah states:

﴾*He who obeys the Messenger has obeyed Allah; but those who turn away - We have not sent you over them as a guardian.*﴿

[*Surah* Nisa:80]

And Allah states:

﴾*O you who have believed, obey Allah and obey the Messenger and those in authority among you. And if you disagree over anything, refer it to Allah and the Messenger, if you should believe in Allah and the Last Day. That is the best [way] and best in result.*﴿ [*Surah* Nisa:59]

Of the greatest signs that indicates the infallibility (ʿ*ismah*) of the Chosen One (the *Mustafa*) (Allah bless and give peace to him and his family) is Allah's protecting him and safeguarding him, as Allah states:

﴾*Indeed, those who pledge allegiance to you, [O Prophet] - they are actually pledging allegiance to Allah. The Hand of Allah is over their hands. So he who breaks his word only breaks it to the detriment of himself. And he who fulfills that which he has promised Allah - Allah will give him a great reward.*﴿

[*Surah* Fath:10]

And Allah states:

﴾*I swear by the star when it goes down. Your companion [Muhammad] has not strayed, nor has he erred, nor does he speak out of desire. It is naught but revelation that is revealed...*﴿

[*Surah* Najm:1-4]

3. Prophethood is for those who did not taint their īmān with darkness

Allah states in surah Baqarah, in response the request of Prophet Ibrahim, al-Khalil, (upon him be peace) when he requested that the leadership (i.e. Prophethood) also be invested in his offspring:

﴾*And [mention, O Muhammad], when Abraham was tried by his Lord with commands and he fulfilled them. [Allah] said, "Indeed, I will make you a leader for the people." [Abraham] said, "And of my descendants?" [Allah] said, "My covenant does not include the wrongdoers."*﴿

[Surah Baqara:124]

And since every act of disobedience is—at the very least—darkness for man, and every disobedient individual and sinner is an oppressor, as the Quran frequently declares, then the Noble Prophets (upon them be peace) must be blameless and completely innocent of perpetrating any type of oppression and disobedience.

Subtle Intra-Religious Differences regarding Infallibility

The Ummah (in a broad sense) has disagreed over the fine details of infallibility and its various definitions and limits. The Mu'tazilites believed that infallibility was *lutf* or 'divine kindness.' So the Mu'tazilite Qadi 'Abd al-Jabbar mentions in *Sharh usul al-khamsa*, on pg. 519:

> Know that *lutf* or divine kindness is everything that an individual chooses to perform that is obligatory and chooses to avoid that is sinful, or anything that is closer to choosing that which is obligatory or avoiding that which is sinful. The names are differed over—some of them term it *tawfiq* or Allah's enabling-grace, while others term it *'ismah* or infallibility.

Imam al-Amidi states in *al-Muwaqif* on pg. 366:

> Shaykh Abu al-Hasan (i.e. al-Ash'ari) and the Imams among his peers opined that: The proof for infallibility (*'ismah*) is the same proof for enabling-grace (*tawfiq*)—according to what preceded that elucidated its core concept—which also is in accordance with its linguistic meaning. Because Allah's creating the capability for obedience and bringing faith (*īmān*) in Him *necessitates* obedience and bringing faith in Him. And the very concept of obedience *necessitates* the avoidance of disobedience, and the concept of īmān *necessitates* the avoidance of disbelief. Thus, Allah's creating the capability for obedience and īmān is protection from disobedience and disbelief itself. So based upon this, there is nothing preventing the word *'ismah* or infallibility from being applied to the creating of obedience and īmān themselves (within the Prophets ﷷ) because it is mutually exclusive to disobedience and disbelief.

Imam al-'Aḍad al-Ijiy (Allah have mercy on him) states in *Abkar al-afkar* (2/208) on the definition of infallibility:

> Infallibility is that Allah does not create [the ability to] sin in the servant.

The most comprehensive passage on the topic of *'ismah* or infallibility was mentioned by the Sharifan *'Allamah*, Abu'l-Baqa al-Husayni al-Kufi al-Qurami al-Hanafi in his book al-*Kulliyat* on pg. 645:

> Imam Abu Mansur al-Maturidi declares that: "Infallibility does not preclude and remove all hardships and tribulations i.e. tribulations are necessary for the existence of free will (*al-ibtilā' al-muqtaḍā li baqā'*

al-ikhtiyār)." The author of *Bidayah* says that Imam al-Maturidi's statement means that: "Allah does not compel man to obey him, nor does he eliminate his ability [and choice] to sin. Instead, it is *lutf* or divine kindness from Allah that inspires man to do good works, and deters him from evil, while maintaining his freedom to choose; all because of tribulation. And both infallibility and enabling-grace (*'ismah* and *tawfiq*) are subcategories that fall under the broad category of *'atf* or Allah's compassion for his servants.

Insofar as *'ismah* or divine protection for *non-prophets* is concerned, then if a Muslim avoids sin and disobedience, it is termed divine protection or *'ismah*, whereas if he performs acts of obedience, then it is termed enabling-grace (*tawfiq*). But regarding the *'ismah* or infallibility of the Noble Prophets (upon them be peace), it refers to [complete] divine protection for them. First, it refers to Allah's granting them—and them alone—a special gift of possessing the purest of all souls, then granting them extraordinary and phenomenal physical attributes, then granting them divine aid and unwavering confidence. Then, Allah's sending divine tranquility and calmness upon them, and by protecting and insulating their hearts, and granting them *tawfiq*. Moreover, He granted infallibility to the Noble Prophets (upon them be peace) from lying about Allah's Message in revelation regarding matters of divine rulings and other related issues, not personal habitual practices, especially when they did not persist and persevere upon mistakes and errors.

Know that the Noble Prophets (upon them be peace) are perpetually protected from disbelief and shameful deeds that detract from dignity or that suggest any wavering in aspirations, and from being accused of lying. And after being tasked with Prophethood, they are protected from all other major sins—not before it. They are also protected from perpetrating minor sins intentionally—not from minor sins that were harmless and not hurtful, or were committed while misinterpreting the prohibition, or done out of forgetfulness but then warning people about it so that they do not follow them in that immediately after becoming cognisant of its being wrong. As for vile, ignoble, and undignified crimes like stealing a morsel of food, or seeds, or petty things of that nature which demonstrate dishonourable character, then they are categorically protected and safeguarded from such acts. Likewise, they are protected regarding malicious and major crimes such as intentionally gazing at a marriageable woman. The preponderance of our [scholarly] companions maintain that they were not prevented from committing major sins prior to Prophethood, much less minor sins, since this would not infringe on their miraculous nature if it (i.e. the protection) was absent from them before Prophethood, nor is there a super-rational text (i.e. the Quran and Sunnah) to prove otherwise.

The *Rafidah Shia* or the 'Rejectionists' maintain that Prophets are infallible and protected from lying and disobedience—without any restrictions or exceptions—minor and major sins, whether intentional or unintentional, before Prophethood and after it; this is disbelief because it contradicts certain texts. The proof that the Prophet ﷺ resembles his *Ummah* in their ability to commit acts of disobedience is Allah saying: ﴿*Say, "I am only a man like you, to whom has been revealed that your god is one God*﴾ (Kahf:110) and Allah says: ﴿*And if We had not strengthened you, you would have almost inclined to them a little*﴾ (Isra:74). However, Allah divinely protected them from inwardly and outwardly committing and adopting prohibited acts at all times, in all places and in all situations. For their rank requires ***ṣidq*** or for them to be truthful in what they convey about Allah by the consensus of scholars. Hence, ***kidhb*** or lying about revelation—whether about rulings or otherwise—is impossible for them. They must also possess ***amāna*** or being trustworthy, according to the well-known opinion. Hence, ***khiyāna*** or treachery by committing something which categorically prohibited or even somewhat discouraged. Rather, what is correct is that they possessed all of these traits both prior to Prophethood and after it. Lying about Allah's Message whether intentionally, forgetfully, or mistakenly is impossible for them. Similarly, it is also impossible for them to do ***kitmān*** or to conceal something which they were obligated to convey.

Thereafter, know that regarding anything connected to Islamic Sacred Law (Sharia) and its injunctions, and anything related to that like teaching the *Ummah* through practical demonstration—they are divinely protected (*ma'sum*) from forgetfulness and mistakes. As for those things that are unrelated to these two categories—and I mean by that anything involving *what* they conveyed of Allah's Message—then indeed, Allah granted each of the Noble Prophets (upon them be peace) specific religious rites and practices, as well as unique individual personalities, temperaments, and thought-processes by which they carried out the particular affairs of their religions *for which they are not taken to task.* Because as regards to that human aspect, they are like other human beings that sometimes forget and err. This is what the bulk of scholars maintain, in contrast to a group of the Sufis and a group of the theologians (*mutakallmin*) who maintain that it is not permissible for Prophets—as a collective—to be unmindful, forgetful, heedless, or err because of their rank. As for some fictitious incidents that are related about them, then what is related with an *āhād* chain or by only one narrator or via only one route of transmission, it is

> obligatory to reject it, because ascribing a mistake to a narrator is far easier than ascribing disobedience to the Noble Prophets of Allah (upon them be peace). As for what is [absurdly] ascribed to them via *tawatur* or mass-transmission, then provided that there is another interpretation, then we interpret it accordingly. And in accordance to the concept of infallibility, we interpret it beyond its superficial and ostensible meaning. And what we find that has no other interpretation and is unavoidable, then we declare it to be before Prophethood, because they were shown, in some extremely rare cases, to commit disobedience, like the brothers of Yusuf who later were tasked with Prophethood.[2] Or *'ismah* can apply to *tark al-awla* which means leaving something supremely virtuous for something virtuous, or it can apply to minor sins committed forgetfully. It can also apply if they committed something then realized it and immediately admitted that it was wrong, or in order to display humbleness, forbearance and temporary compliance [to achieve a higher objective], and the are other plausible considerations.

Perhaps the original, comprehensive definition that preceded and that we mentioned summarizes the various opinions of the scholars. The upshot is that *'ismah* or infallibility refers to protection from Allah from anything that would detract and sully the good reputation of a Prophet. And a Prophet is *mukallaf* or accountable before Allah and he is bound by the dictates and conditions of *taklif* or accountability like any other person. However, he enjoys the highest level of divine protection from Allah that comes between him and disobedience which would sully [the credence of] his message. One should keep in mind that the protection (*'ismah*) of a Prophet includes divine accountability while maintaining free will to choose, which is dissimilar to the restrictive type of *'ismah* held by the Angels who do not have free will, as Allah says:

﴿*The Angels do not disobey Allah in what He commands them but do what they are commanded.*﴾

[Surah Tahrim:6]

Moreover, because of a concatenation of Quranic verses, reports,

---

[2] There is nothing explicit in the Quran nor the Sunna affirming this. Thus, they are not considered of the twenty-five Quranic Prophets nor of those about whom there is a significant difference of opinion over whether or not they are Prophets like Khidr, Luqman, Maryam (upon them all be peace), for example. However, some scholars have mentioned this position based on Judaeo-Christian reports, and Allah knows best. [t]

and indications (*isharat*), I personally believe that the *'ismah* or protection granted to the Noble Prophets and Messengers (upon them be peace) is far greater and superior than that given to those who convey the messages on behalf of the Prophets. So Messengers (*rusul*) are granted a *Risala* or Sacred Law whereas a Prophet (*nabi*) is commanded to spread the Sacred Law of a previous prophet.

Beyond that, the *'ismah* of the Five Prophets of Firm Resolve[3] (*Ulu'l 'azmi min al-rusul*) is greater than the *'ismah* of the other Noble Prophets and Messengers (upon them all be peace), because they are exemplars, paragons, and set the standard for all else. And above and beyond that, the *'ismah* of the Noblest and Greatest Prophet (*Nabi al-Akram wa Rasul al-'Azam*), Prophet Muhammad (Allah bless and give peace to him and his family), is infinitely greater and infinitely more perfect than the rest of his brothers among the *Ulu'l 'azmi min al-rusul*. This is because he is the Ultimate Criterion and the Supreme Standard (*al-Mizan al-Muhaymin*), the Greatest Role Model (*al-Qudwa al-'Uzma*), the Standard-Bearer of Praise on the Day of Judgment, and the Intercessor whose intercession is accepted that Day, as Allah says:

❮*And [recall, O People of the Scripture], when Allah took the covenant of the prophets, [saying], "Whatever I give you of the Scripture and wisdom and then there comes to you a messenger confirming what is with you, you [must] believe in him and support him." [Allah] said, "Have you acknowledged and taken upon that My commitment?" They said, "We have acknowledged it." He said, "Then bear witness, and I am with you among the witnesses."*❯

[Surah Al-'Imran:81]

This verse necessitates [and logically implies] that the greatest protection and infinite preservation is afforded to our Prophet Muhammad (Allah bless and give peace to him and his family) [since Allah ordered them to believe in and support him, whereas he was not commanded to do the same for them], and Allah knows best.

Authorship on the Infallibility of the Prophets

It is said that the first to author a work on *'ismah* is the Shi'ite, Sharif Murtada (d. 436 *hijri*), whose has a book which he titled **Tanzīh al-anbiyā'** (*The Impeccability of the Prophets*) in which he appended a portion

---

[3] *Ulu'l 'azmi min al-rusul* or the Five Prophets of Firm Resolve are (in descending rank): Our Master, Sayyiduna Muhammad (Allah bless and give peace to him and his family), Prophets 'Isa, Musa, Ibrahim, and Nuh (upon them all be peace). [t]

on the infallibility of the Twelve Imams in his book after the topic of the infallibility of the Prophets to support and promote his ideology of the Twelve Imams. And the Mu'tazilite Judge, 'Abd al-Jabbar al-Hamdani (d. 415 *hijri*), pointed out in *Tathbit dala'il al-nabuwwah* that the Twelver Shi'ite, Hisham b. al-Hakam al-Kindi, the bondsman of Banu Shayban (d. 199 *hijri*), was the first to discuss '*ismah* or infallibility and that it was not well-known in the era of the *Tabi'in* (the Followers) and the *Taba' tabi'in* (the Successors to the Followers) and those preceding them.

Thereafter, the erudite Imam who died year 606 *hijri*, Fakhr al-Din al-Razi (Allah have mercy upon him), penned his work ***'Ismah al-anbiyā'*** (The Infallibility of the Prophets) which is a masterpiece on the self-same topic. It furnishes proofs to establish the infallibility of the Noble Prophets (upon them be peace) and refutes obfuscations surrounding the topic, as he did in his monumental tafsir entitled *Tafsir al-Kabir* by elucidating and demystifying Quranic verses that are often misinterpreted to contradict the notion of infallibility.

Except that 'Allamah, Shaykh, Nur al-Din Ahmad b. Mahmud al-Sabuni (d. 580 *hijri*) authored a book entitled ***Muntaqā fi 'ismah al-anbiyā'***. This Shaykh Nur al-Din was a contemporary of Imam al-Razi and opposed him in three pivotal issues between the Maturidis and the Ash'aris, namely, 1) the Beatific Vision (*ru'yatullah*), 2) *takwin* (a semantic theological point), and 3) *Baqa'* or the Prophets remaining preserved in their graves, as mentioned in *Munadharat Fakhr al-Din al-Razi fi bilad ma wara' al-nahar*. Shaykh Nur al-Din al-Sabuni's book *Muntaqa fi 'ismah al-anbiya* is a summary of Shaykh Abu'l-Husayn Muhammad b. Yahya al-Bashaghouri's ***Kashf al-ghawāmiḍ fi aḥwāl al-anbiyā'*** which is also known as '*Ismah al-anbiya*. This Shaykh Abu'l-Husayn al-Bashaghouri died at the end of the fourth century *hijri*. Shaykh Nur al-Din al-Sabuni mentions that no one ever wrote a book on this topic before and he mentioned in his book *Muntaqa fi 'ismah al-anbiya*, pg. 5:

> Shaykh Abu'l-Husayn al-Bashaghouri said: "I heard Shaykh Abu'l-Hasan al-Rustufghini (d. 345 *hijri*), may Allah have mercy on him, saying: 'Someone wrote a book in the era of Shaykh Abu Mansur al-Maturidi (d. 333 *hijri*) titled *Kitab ma'asi al-anbiya* (On the Disobedience of the Prophets), so Shaykh Abu Mansur remarked: 'Indeed, this author—based on the obvious intent of his work—has committed disbelief (*kafara*), because [logically] whoever authors any book intends to find as much as he can [on the topic] and vigorously inspects, checks, and researches the topic with due diligence to present a thorough

> analysis. And [generally] whoever searches out and hopes to find the disobedience of a believer, it is feared he will lose his Īmān. So if this is the case with a believer, then what will be the outcome of someone who takes it upon himself to seek out the so-called 'disobediences' of a Messenger to publicize it?' As a result, Shaykh Abu'l-Husayn al-Bashaghouri (Allah have mercy upon him) authored his own book which he called *'Ismah al-anbiya.*'"

Thereafter came 'Allamah Abu'l-Hasan b. Ahmad al-Sibty al-Umawi, famously known as Ibn Khumayr (d. 614 *hijri*), with his book ***Tanzīh al-anbiyā' 'amma nasaba ilayhim ḥathalātu al-aghbiyā'***. It refutes some of the obfuscations that were raised against the infallibility of the Noble Prophets (upon them be peace) and has been printed with editing by our Shaykh, the *'Allamah*, the *Muhaddith*, the Sharifan, Muhammad Ibrahim 'Abd al-Ba'ith al-Sikandari (Allah have mercy upon him). All the books that came after them are comparable and similar to them, and Allah knows best.

Conclusion

Allah has ennobled humanity by sending His Beloved Messengers to them, and opened an enormous door by which they can enter into His Proximity, Love, Mercy, and Forgiveness by following the Beloved Messengers. Allah states on the tongue of Prophet 'Isa (upon him be peace):

﴾*I said not to them except what You commanded me - to worship Allah, my Lord and your Lord. And I was a witness over them as long as I was among them; but when You took me up, You were the Observer over them, and You are, over all things, Witness. If You should punish them - indeed they are Your servants; but if You forgive them - indeed it is You who is the Exalted in Might, the Wise.*﴿

[Maida:117-118]

As well, Allah said on the tongue of Prophet Ibrahim (upon whom be peace):

﴾*And [mention, O Muhammad], when Abraham said, "My Lord, make this city [Makkah] secure and keep me and my sons away from worshipping idols. My Lord, indeed they have led astray many among the people. So whoever follows me - then he is of me; and whoever disobeys me - indeed, You are [yet] Forgiving and Merciful.*﴿

[Surah Ibrahim:35-36]

To conclude, I would like to touch on the point of *Baqā'* or the bodies of the Noble Prophets (upon them be peace) not decomposing in their graves—especially the final Prophet, our Master Muhammad (Allah bless and give peace to him and his family). The Quran elucidates to us that the very presence of our Master Muhammad (Allah bless and give peace to him and his family) among us is the cause and reason that calamities and punishments are warded off and kept at bay. Allah states:

﴾*But Allah would not punish them while you [O Prophet] are among them, and Allah would not punish them while they seek forgiveness.*﴿

[Surah Anfal:33]

This is substantiated by the words of the Prophet (Allah bless and give peace to him and his family):

I was only sent as a mercy. (Muslim 2601)

In addition, Allah alerted us to the immensity of the blessing upon us, as Allah states:

﴾*Certainly did Allah confer an unrepayable favor upon the believers when He sent among them a Messenger from themselves, reciting to them His verses and purifying them and teaching them the Book and wisdom, although they had been before in manifest error.*﴿

[Surah Al-'Imran:164]

Allah also states:

﴾*Indeed, We have sent you as a witness and a bringer of good tidings and a warner. That you [people] may believe in Allah and His Messenger and honor him and respect the Prophet and exalt Allah morning and afternoon.*﴿

[Surah Fath:8-9]

So all praise belongs to Allah, Lord of the Worlds.

Written while praising Allah and sending peace and blessings upon His Prophet ﷺ:

(Shaykh) Muhammad b. Yahya b. Muhammad al-Ninowy
Rajab al-Murajjab 1438 AH / April 2017 CE
May Allah forgive him.

Chapter One

The Infallibility of the Prophets

Of the things that distinguish the Prophets over the rest of mankind is being far removed from disobedience, untouched by blameworthy desires, and aversion to anything that would detract from manhood, invalidate honour, or diminish the respect of a man. The Prophets are the most perfect of people in character, the purest of them in deeds and in soul, and have the most fragrant of biographies, because they are role-models for mankind and are beautiful exemplars for humanity. So for this reason, Allah commanded us to emulate them, imitate their manners, and follow their way in all aspects of life. Allah said:

﴿أُولَٰئِكَ الَّذِينَ هَدَى اللَّهُ ۖ فَبِهُدَاهُمُ اقْتَدِهْ ۗ﴾

﴿*Those were the (Prophets) who received Allah's guidance: Emulate the guidance they received.*﴾

[Surah An'ām 6:90]

﴿لَقَدْ كَانَ لَكُمْ فِي رَسُولِ اللَّهِ أُسْوَةٌ حَسَنَةٌ﴾

﴿*Ye have indeed in the Messenger of Allah a beautiful pattern (of conduct).*﴾

[Surah Aḥzāb 33:21]

The Definition of Infallibility

The Arabic word ''*iṣmah*' or infallibility linguistically means prevention. So it is said in Arabic: '*I prevented him* ('*aṣimtuhu*) from the food' i.e. I prevented him from partaking in the food. Or '*I prevented him* ('*aṣimtuhu*) from lying' i.e. I stopped him from it.

Also, Allah Most High's Word [about Prophet Nuh's son]:

﴿قَالَ سَآوِي إِلَىٰ جَبَلٍ يَعْصِمُنِي مِنَ الْمَاءِ ۚ﴾

﴿*But he said, "I will take refuge on a mountain to protect me (ya'ṣimunī) from the water.*﴾

[Surah Hud 11:43]

i.e. the mountain will prevent me from drowning.

Allah Most High's statement [from Zulaykha, the minister's wife's declaration about Prophet Yusuf ﷺ]:

﴿ وَلَقَدْ رَاوَدْتُهُ عَنْ نَفْسِهِ فَاسْتَعْصَمَ ﴾

﴾*And I certainly sought to seduce him, but he firmly refused ('fa 'taṣama).*﴿

[Surah Yusuf 12:32]

In addition, the Prophet Muhammad ﷺ states in the following *hadith:*

> I was ordered to fight against the people until they bear witness there is no god but Allah, and if they do that, they have protected (*'aṣamū*) their blood and their wealth from me—except what relates to the criminal code in Islam, and their ultimate reckoning is with Allah.

Imam Qurṭubī ﷺ said, "Infallibility in Arabic is called *'iṣmah* because it prevents from committing disobedience."

According to the Sacred law, infallibility is Allah's protection of His Prophets and Messengers ﷺ from falling into sins, disobedience, committing evil deeds and prohibited acts. Infallibility has been firmly established for Prophets and is one of their traits[4] which Allah Most High has honoured and distinguished them with over the rest of humanity. This does not apply to anyone save the Noble Prophets ﷺ such that Allah has gifted them exclusively with this magnificent blessing, and guarded them from committing acts of disobedience and sins, both minor and major. Thus, it is not possible for them to fall into disobedience or act contrary to the orders of Allah ﷻ which sets them apart from the rest of humanity.

The wisdom behind that is Allah ﷻ has commanded us to emulate them and to follow in their footsteps for they are the beautiful role-models and righteous examples for creation, and the embodiment of human perfection for the entire human race. Were they permitted to fall into acts of disobedience or to commit deadly sins and vice, then either disobedience would have become legislated for us or it would not have been obligatory to obey them, and neither of these two cases

---

[4] Muslim theologians have averred that Prophets ﷺ have four necessary traits, four impossible traits, and one possible trait. The four necessary and impossible traits are respectively 1) truthfulness and lying 2) high intelligence and dim-wittedness 3) trustworthiness and treachery 4) conveying the message and concealing the message. They have one possible trait which is 5) any human conditions that do not detract from human dignity. (*Bajūrī, Risalat fil 'ilm al-Tawḥīd*)

are rational. Rather, they are impossible because they are the leaders of humanity, and how can a leader command to virtue and prohibit the immoral, then act to the contrary and commit the very same vice and act of immorality? Moreover, what are acts of disobedience and sins other than spiritual filth that is akin to physical filth and disease? So how could it be conceivable to attribute such things to the Noble Prophets and Messengers ﷺ?

The following words of the Prophet ﷺ indicate that disobedience (*ma ʿṣiyah*) is an internal type of filth:

> Whoever amongst you is put to trial with the least of these [spiritual] diseases should conceal it because whoever exposes it to us, then we will establish the decree of Allah.

This or similar wordings have been transmitted. Meaning, whoever exposes his disobedience and announces it must have the legal Islamic punishment applied upon him. Thus, both logic and the Sharia necessitate the belief in the infallibility of Prophets ﷺ for how could it be possible for one to simultaneously be a Prophet and a thief, or a highway robber, or a consumer of intoxicants, or a fornicator, or a perpetrator of other filthy spiritual diseases which would prevent others from emulating or following them? And will speech have an effect on the souls of other people if one's own life is not righteous or one's life is sullied by deadly sins and inequities?

Therefore, it is imperative for the life of a Prophet to be a noble and virtuous one, illumined with the light of guidance, known for chastity and purity, abound with virtue, nobility, and piety. *This* is what is called infallibility of the Prophets ﷺ!

The following quote is mentioned in the book entitled *Islamic Creed* (*ʿAqīda al-Islāmīyya*) in the chapter regarding infallibility:

> It is established that the Messenger ﷺ is the loftiest example among his Community (*Ummah*) and it is obligatory to follow his beliefs, acts, words, and manners. Since he is a beautiful example for us to emulate by the testimony of Allah for him[5] – except for what is included in his exclusive qualities (*khasa'is*) by explicit text – it is obligatory that all of his beliefs, works, words and his volitional manners - after receiving the Message – be in accordance with the obedience of Allah Most High. And it would be obligatory for not even the most miniscule part of his beliefs, works, statements and manners to be admixed with the

[5] The Quran declares: ﴾*Indeed, for you, in the Messenger of Allah, is a most beautiful example...*﴿ (*Ahzab 33:21*)

disobedience of Allah because Allah ﷻ has commanded the various communities to emulate their respective Messengers. So, were it possible for the Messengers to commit acts of disobedience after receiving the Message, it would undermine the whole notion of taking them as role models since we are commanded to emulate all of their acts, and if we assume for the sake of argument, that they perpetrated acts of disobedience – that would implicitly be a command for us to perform acts of disobedience; and that is a clear contradiction.

Allah's Protection for His Prophet Muhammad ﷺ Since Childhood

Allah Most High has protected our Prophet ﷺ since his childhood and safeguarded him from the deeds of the Age of Ignorance (*Jāhilīyyah*) in his childhood, his youth, and right up to his being commissioned with Prophethood. Accordingly, the blessing of Divine protection from sin was completed for him by being commissioned to bear the responsibility of conveying the Prophetic Message in the most complete and perfect way.

Ibn Hishām ﵀ said in his *Sīrah al-nabawīyyah* (*Prophetic Biography*):

> Allah Most High provided the Messenger of Allah ﷺ an upbringing under His guardianship and safeguarded him from the diseases of the Age of Ignorance because of the nobility and the Message that Allah had intended for him, up until he reached manhood. He was the most superior of his people in manhood, the most excellent of them in character, the noblest of them in lineage, the most excellent of the them in neighbourliness, the greatest of them in forbearance, the most truthful of them in speech, the greatest of them in keeping trusts, the furthest of them from obscenity and conduct which defiles the integrity and nobility of men. To the extent, that he did not have an appellation among his people except 'the trustworthy' because of what Allah gathered in him of righteous traits.

According to my knowledge – the Messenger of Allah ﷺ spoke about how Allah protected him in his childhood in the Pre-Islamic Age of Ignorance when he ﷺ said:

> You would have seen me among the young boys of Quraysh; we were moving stones and would play the way boys would play with them while all of us were uncovered. We would put our wraparound (*izār*) on our shoulders to carry the stones on it, and I would go and come with them. When suddenly someone struck me with a painful blow and said: 'Tie your *izār* properly!' So I took it and properly tied it on myself among my friends.

Suhaylī 🙵 said commenting on this story:

> This story was narrated in a hadith at the time of the re-building of the Ka'ba. The Messenger of Allah 🙵 would move the stones with his people to the Ka'ba and they would place their wraparound (*izār*) on their shoulders to protect themselves from the stones. The Messenger of Allah 🙵 would carry them on his shoulders while his *izār* was tied properly on him. 'Abbās 🙵 said to him: 'O nephew, if you put your *izār* on your shoulder [it would be better for you to carry the stones].' He 🙵 then did so and fell unconscious. Then he 🙵 said: 'My *izār*! My *izār*!', then fastened his *izār*, stood up and began carrying the stones again.

And the *hadith* of Ibn Isḥāq in this regard, if it was authentic, states that this occurred in his childhood and this occurred a total of two times; once in his childhood and another as a young man 🙵.

Chapter Two

Does Infallibility Apply Before or After Prophethood?

Scholars differed over whether or not the infallibility of Prophets ﷺ applies before or after Prophethood, and also over whether they are only divinely protected from major sins, or from both major *and* minor sins.

Some scholars concluded that infallibility is established for them before Prophethood *and* after it because a Prophet's manners – even before Prophethood – have an influence on his future summoning to Allah. Thus, it is necessary for them to possess an upright lifestyle and a pure soul to ensure nothing could discredit their Message and their summoning (*da'wah*) to Allah.

The proof for that is Allah, Blessed and Exalted is He, has selected His Prophets from amongst the elite of mankind and has nurtured them since their childhood under His special care as He said to Prophet Mūsā ﷺ:

﴿ وَلِتُصْنَعَ عَلَى عَيْنِي ﴾

﴿*... that you would be brought up under My special care.*﴾

[Surah Ṭāhā 20:39]

And He made them among the elect:

﴿ وَإِنَّهُمْ عِندَنَا لَمِنَ الْمُصْطَفَيْنَ الْأَخْيَارِ ﴾

﴿*And indeed they are, to Us, among the elect and outstanding.*﴾

[Surah Ṣād 38:47]

Therefore, it is imperative that they be divinely protected and safeguarded both preceding Prophethood and after it.

As for the second group of scholars, they concluded that the infallibility of the Prophets ﷺ is exclusively after Prophethood and it is from both minor and major sins because humanity is not commanded to follow them before Prophethood. Thus, following the Prophets and emulating their example only applies *after* revelation descends upon them and after their bearing the Message and Trust of Islam.

As for before it, they are akin to the rest of mankind. Yet, in spite of that, their pure lives do not allow them to accept falling into disobedience, vice or deviance by means of obscenity or base actions because even if they were not infallible before Prophethood, they are nonetheless granted a great fortune of divine concern and primordial nature.

The following passage has been related in the book '*Islamic Creed and its Foundations*':

> "...before being selected for Prophethood, a prophet can be viewed in two ways:
>
> 1. He was either not yet specifically commissioned with a specific law. Hence, infallibility, in his case, is not applicable because disobedience and violations only apply after the coming of a Sacred Law and being charged to follow it, and it is more likely that he was not yet responsible for a Sacred Law. Hence, there is no room for investigating 'infallibility' or 'fallibility' because blameworthiness is only applicable when there is accountability.
>
> Nevertheless, the lofty primordial nature of a Messenger, the purity of his character, his exalted soul, and the soundness of his intelligence predicates his being an immaculate example among his people in his character, his interactions, his trustworthiness, and his remoteness from committing obnoxious deeds which are deemed repulsive by sound intellects and upright natures.
>
> 2. As for the case of being responsible to follow a prior messenger's Sacred Law like the case of our Master Lūṭ ﷺ when, before his own Prophethood, he was following his paternal uncle Ibrahim ﷺ, and similarly is the case of the Prophets of the Children of Israel after Mūsā ﷺ as they were charged to follow his Sacred Law before their Prophethood was revealed to them.[6] This circumstance does not have conclusive proof regarding the infallibility of Prophets, neither from major sins nor minor sins. However the lives of the Prophets ﷺ—that which is authentically transmitted about them *before* their respective prophethoods—bear testimony that they were the furthest of people from acts of disobedience, whether major or minor.
>
> Were the slightest of those things to emanate from them, it would be an extremely rare slip, and it would not discredit them due to their lofty primordial nature, their pure character, elevated souls, and due

[6] Such as Prophets Yaḥyā and Zakariyya, or Yūsha and Mūsā ﷺ.

to their mission which would be commissioned to them later on in life.

These rare mistakes would only emanate from them for two reasons. Firstly, to establish their 'humanness' in front of creation, so that creation does not raise them beyond their human rank, nor to elevate them into possessing God-like traits, which would be impossible to be ascribed to them. Hence, they are in reality but noble, created servants belonging to Allah Most High. And secondly, in order to manifest the difference between their states before Prophethood and their states after it.[7]

Therefore, among these scholarly opinions, the correct and relied upon position is that the Prophets (peace and blessings of Allah be upon them) are divinely protected from sins, both major and minor, after Prophethood by consensus. As for being protected before Prophethood, it is conceivable that some minor infractions may have occurred from them which do not take away from nobility nor detract from their honour and dignity.

ʿAllāmah Qurṭubī said in his *Tafsir Jāmiʿ li ahkām al-Quran*:

> After scholars have unanimously agreed that the Prophets are divinely protected from major sins, and from every base act containing disgrace and deficiency by consensus, they differed as to whether Prophets can commit minor sins. The preponderance of jurists aver that they are divinely protected from all minor sins identical to their Divine protection from all major sins because our being commanded to emulate their acts, footsteps and their way of life is an unconditional command; no restrictions apply. So if we were to conceive that they could commit minor sins, then it would be impossible to emulate them since we would then not be able to discern whether any of their actions would be classified under the Islamic ruling of 'gaining nearness to Allah,' permissible, prohibited, or disobedience. And it is inappropriate to instruct someone to fulfil a command if it may very well be an act of disobedience.

Abu Isḥāq al-Asfarāyanī, one of the scholars from the Sunni tradition said:

> Sins do not emanate from the Prophets because they are divinely protected from major and minor sins, and that is a definitive proof of their miraculous nature. Some said minor sins can occur from them, but there is no basis for this position. And the majority of scholars hold that that it is impossible for them.

---

[7] *ʿAqīda al-Islāmīyya* by Ustadh Habanka pg. 116

Some of the later scholars said:

> What is befitting to say is Allah Most High has declared that small mistakes have occurred with some of them; He attributed it to them and censured them about it. They disclosed that about themselves, rid themselves of it, felt fearful about it and repented. And none of this detracts from their lofty status; rather it only occurred as a minor mistake and out of forgetfulness. So, in relation to anyone besides them, it is deemed a good deed. But for those of their high status, it is considered a bad deed.

Junayd [al-Baghdādī, the master of jurisprudence and *Sufism*] ﷺ put it beautifully when he said:

(حَسَنَاتُ الْأَبْرَارِ سَيِّئَاتُ الْمُقَرَّبِينَ)

(ḥasanāt al-'abrār siyyi'āt al-muqarrabīn)

"The good deeds of the pious are the bad deeds for those brought-nigh."

It is also said: 'A political ambassador is held responsible for what an average labourer would be rewarded for.'[8]

Imam al-Qurṭubī ﷺ said:

> This is the absolute truth because for them ﷺ, regardless if the texts apparently give the impression that sins have occurred from them, this does not detract from their rank nor diminish their station. Rather, Allah has corrected them, chose them, guided them, purified them, selected them, and elected them (may the blessings of Allah be upon them and His peace).

(Tafsir al-Qurṭubī, vol. 1, pg. 308)

Does Infallibility Apply to Non-Prophets?

Infallibility does not apply to anyone other than the Noble Prophets ﷺ since every other individual is susceptible to mistakes, misguidance, and falling into disobedience. However, Allah ﷻ has protected some of His saints from major sins and safeguarded them from immoral acts by way of Divine Protection and Divine Support. This is due to Godly Kindness, not from 'Divine Protection' which Allah designates

---

[8] That is, the more authority and responsibility with which one has been entrusted, the higher the standard one will be expected to maintain, or in other words, with great power comes great responsibility.

exclusively to His Messengers and His Prophets ﷺ.

Allah Most High says:

﴿ يَا أَيُّهَا الَّذِينَ آمَنُوا اتَّقُوا اللَّهَ وَآمِنُوا بِرَسُولِهِ يُؤْتِكُمْ كِفْلَيْنِ مِنْ رَحْمَتِهِ وَيَجْعَلْ لَكُمْ نُورًا تَمْشُونَ بِهِ وَيَغْفِرْ لَكُمْ وَاللَّهُ غَفُورٌ رَحِيمٌ ﴾

❴O you who have believed! Fear Allah and believe in His Messenger; He will then give you a double portion of His mercy and make for you <u>a light</u> by which you will walk and forgive you; and Allah is Forgiving and Merciful.❵

[Surah Ḥadīd 57:28]

The *'light'* in the above Quranic verse refers to the Divine Kindness that is granted to the saints and the God-fearing, or the veracious. Again it is from Divine Preservation and Divine support, not infallibility.

There are some of the Noble Companions whom Allah has distinguished with that Divine bounty such as Abu Bakr ؓ and ʿUmar ؓ. The Prophet ﷺ has informed that Allah had made truth manifest on the tongue of ʿUmar ؓ and his heart. And he ﷺ said to ʿUmar ؓ:

(وَالَّذِي نَفْسِي بِيَدِهِ مَا رَآكَ الشَّيْطَانُ سَالِكًا فَجًّا إِلَّا سَلَكَ فَجًّا غَيْرَ فَجِّكَ يَا عُمَرُ)

I swear by the One in whose hand is my soul, Satan does not see you taking one pathway save he will take another path other than your path, O ʿUmar.

The claim of some dissenters that some ordinary people have Divine protection has no basis nor is there proof to substantiate it from The Book and the *Sunna*. It is mere delusions and dreams. Sinlessness is for none save the Prophets ﷺ because Allah has ordained them to be exemplars for the universe as Allah Most High has stated:

﴿ وَجَعَلْنَاهُمْ أَئِمَّةً يَهْدُونَ بِأَمْرِنَا وَأَوْحَيْنَا إِلَيْهِمْ فِعْلَ الْخَيْرَاتِ وَإِقَامَ الصَّلَاةِ وَإِيتَاءَ الزَّكَاةِ وَكَانُوا لَنَا عَابِدِينَ ﴾

❴And We made them leaders, guiding by Our Command, and We sent them inspiration to do good deeds, to establish regular prayers, and to practise regular charity; and they constantly served Us.❵

[Surah Anbiyāʾ 21:73]

Every human being, except for the Noble Prophets ﷺ, is susceptible to mistakes. To this, Imam Malik ؓ said:

(مَا مِنَّا إِلَّا مَنْ رَدَّ وَرُدَّ عَلَيْهِ، إِلَّا صَاحِبُ هَذَا الْقَبْرِ)

'There is no one amongst us except he refutes and is refuted save the person in this grave.'

By that he meant the Prophet ﷺ because of his Divine Protection.

The Belief of the People of the Book about the Prophets عليهم السلام

So the abovementioned Islamic perspective—a dignified perspective—holds that the most pristine of reputations and the embodiment of all human perfection is found in none other than the Noble Prophets عليهم السلام. They are the role models, exemplars, leaders, and guides for mankind, which the Quran corroborates and describes as such. However, in contrast to this, we find that the beliefs of the People of the Book transgress all bounds and malign the integrity of the pure Prophets عليهم السلام. They do not suffice in ascribing disobedience to them or in denying their infallibility. Rather, they depict some of them to be the champions of crime, the leaders of corruption and licentiousness, and the perpetrators of the greatest sins.

You find in the Torah - the altered version, of course - many such mortifying things including that one of the Prophets, namely Prophet Lūṭ عليه السلام, drank alcohol then shared the bed with his two daughters (i.e. he had intercourse with them after becoming inebriated) and they both became pregnant from him via incest. I seek forgiveness from Allah! Which crime is uglier than this foul indecency, saying that a Prophet would commit the crime of incest with his two daughters after getting drunk from alcohol? How heinous and repulsive an accusation!

The only reason we are transmitting the text which is recorded in the Torah is to clarify to the reader the beliefs of the Jews about the Prophets عليهم السلام, the extent of the fabrication and slander the Jews have attached to them as compared to what we (Muslims) affirm and confidently assert are fabricated stories about the Noble Prophets عليهم السلام, and that these are from the alterations to the original Book of Allah.

The following quote has been narrated in *The Book of Genesis* on page 128:

> Lut ascended the mountains and took repose there with his two daughters because he was fearful of living in *Ṣāghir*. He and his two daughters took refuge in a cave.
>
> Then the older daughter said to the younger daughter, 'our father has

aged and there is no man on earth that can have relations with us. So come, we will get him drunk, share the bed with him and we will beget offspring for our father.'

So they gave their father alcohol to drink that night and the eldest daughter shared the bed with her father while he was actually unaware of sharing the bed with his daughter and when she arose from the bed.

When the next day came, the eldest daughter said to the youngest, 'It worked. I shared the bed last night with our father. So we should give him alcohol to drink tonight, too. Go to him and share the bed with him so we can beget offspring from our father.'

Thus, they gave their father alcohol to drink that night also and the youngest went to her father and shared the bed with her father. He did not know that he shared the bed with her nor when she arose.

Thus, the two daughters of Lūt were impregnated by their father. The eldest daughter gave birth to a boy named 'Moab' and he is the father of the 'Moabites' until this day. And the youngest daughter also gave birth to a boy name 'Ammon' and he is the father of the 'Ammonites' until today.

In addition we find the following in the 38th chapter of *The Book of Genesis* on page 128:

> Judah son of Jacob (Yaqub) committed fornication with his son's wife and she became pregnant with his illegitimate child and begot twins (Perez and Zerah).

And as explicitly stated in the first chapter of the New Testament of Matthew, Dawud ﷺ, Sulaymān ﷺ and 'Īsā are all the progeny of Perez, and that Dawud ﷺ committed fornication with the wife of Uriah, the commanding officer of his army, and she became pregnant from him by fornication. So Dawud ﷺ treacherously killed her husband [Uriah] and took her as a wife as is explicitly mentioned in chapter 11 of the '*Book of Samuel*'. (11 Samuel, 11)[9]

However, there is something that is still more disastrous and bitter than this since the Jews assert that Prophet Sulaymān ﷺ committed apostasy at the end of his life and he used to worship idols after his apostasy, and he built several temples for them which are mentioned in the eleventh chapter of the first '*Book of Kings*.' (1 Kings, 1)

---

[9] The translator has added a section in this book from another book by Imam al-Ṣābūnī entitled *Ṣafwat al-Tafāsīr* addressing this very story that has been incorrectly included in some books of *tafsīr*. It violates the concept of infallibility and has been shown to be from a false Judeo-Christian report (*Isra'īlīyāt*).

Good Lord! What sanctity is left for the Prophets ﷺ? How would it be possible to follow them if this was their history i.e. drunkenness, evil character, fornication, shedding blood, and worshipping idols?

These are only some of the beliefs of the Jews about their Prophets; all of them are lies, false testimony, and slander. We Muslims categorically denounce all of those claims and their ilk as untrue and from the alterations of the Jews, not the Torah that Allah revealed upon Mūsā ﷺ.

As for the Christians, they do not believe in the infallibility of Prophets. That is based upon their belief of the Divine nature of the Master, the Messiah 'Īsā ﷺ, because, according to them, he is the only one who is infallible and the rest of humanity, including the Prophets, commit sins. They believe there is no one who can be an intercessor nor saviour save the Messiah because 'a sinner cannot save other sinners,' according to the wording in the Gospel.

Christians also hold demeaning views about the Prophets that are no less despicable than those of the Jews. Both of them accuse the Prophets of committing sins and perpetrating crimes which are neither accepted by logic nor a divinely transmitted text.

The late Shaykh Muhammad Rāshid Riḍā ؒ said the following quote in his book '*Muhammadan Revelation*' (*al-Waḥi al-Muhammadī*):

> If the Prophets were sent to humanity to guide them to purification of the soul, to rectify the condition of their worldly affairs, and to prepare them for the hereafter, then this goal would not be complete except if those Prophets were fit to be emulated in their actions, their way of life, adhering to their respective Sacred Laws and the good manners which they convey on behalf of their Lord.

Thus from this perspective, our scholars declare it to be obligatory for Prophets to be infallible from disobedience and disgraceful acts. Some scholars went to the extent of saying that they are divinely protected from sins, both minor and major, before Prophethood and after it. Some of the scholars have restricted infallibility to minor sins that are spurred by baseness and lowliness.

The People of the Book do not believe in this Divine protection, and their Holy Books accuse some of the eminent Prophets of obscene major sins which invalidate the notion of being a good role-model. Rather, it is in accordance with pure evil and corruption.

Some among the Christians make the 'disobediences' of the Prophets a proof for their belief that only the Messiah is infallible because he is, according to them, the 'Lord and God' and because he is the 'only saviour for humanity' from punishment from the 'original sin' which is attached to every child of Ādam by inheriting it from him, and because there can be no intercessor nor saviour for them except him since 'a sinner cannot save other sinners while he is one of them.' This is a pagan creed which opposes the way of the Prophets and their books, and opposes sound reason, and is actually applied in the idolatrous Indian religions and other like them.

Despite the fact that the Old and New Testament are holy according to them and altered according to us, those books do not support their accusation of sins for all Prophets, not to mention acts of disobedience which are worse than sins because, for example, John the Baptist was never tarnished with sin. On the contrary, their Gospels testify for him with what suggests that he is greater than the Messiah in his infallibility.

In the Gospel of Luke (Luke 1, 5) it states:

> "...that he is great in front of the Lord, and alcohol and intoxicants, he drinketh not, and from the womb of his mother, he was filled with the Holy Spirit."

It also states:

> "...the Hand of the Lord was with him."

And the Messiah said about him:

> "The truth I speaketh unto you. There did not arise from amongst any begotten ones from women, anyone greater than John the Baptist."
>
> (Matthew 11, 11)

On the other hand, the Gospels testify that the Messiah belittled his mother and his brothers and did not permit them to meet him when they sought permission to speak to him. It is stated in the Gospel of Luke (Luke 8, 20-21):

> Some informed him: 'Your mother and brothers are standing outside wishing to see you.' He answered them: 'My mother and my brothers are those who listen to the word of Allah and act according to it.'

Sayyid Rāshid Riḍā says:

> Yes, his brothers did not believe him as is explicitly stated in another

place, but was his mother like that too? Will he treat her with treatment like this?

Allah Most High commands to show excellence to one's parents, whether or not they were idolaters, and He preferred the mother of Master Messiah ʿĪsa over the women of the world [at her time], and dishonouring one's mother is a sin in all religious laws and codes of ethics, so we absolve him [Isa عليه السلام] from all of that.

So in summary, the Muslim belief about the Prophets عليهم السلام is the true belief system that the Quran brought, and their noble and pure lives testify to its veracity. It befits their lofty rank, their sublime status, and the belief of the infallibility of Prophets عليهم السلام entails believing in their pureness and freedom from base qualities. It is what is in accordance with the text of the Quran, which positions them as leaders in this world and the hereafter, and their carrying the Banner of Praise and guidance for the universe. About this, Allah, Sublime is His Praise, states:

﴿ وَجَعَلْنَاهُمْ أَئِمَّةً يَهْدُونَ بِأَمْرِنَا وَأَوْحَيْنَا إِلَيْهِمْ فِعْلَ الْخَيْرَاتِ وَإِقَامَ الصَّلَاةِ وَإِيتَاءَ الزَّكَاةِ ۖ وَكَانُوا لَنَا عَابِدِينَ ﴾

﴿And We made them leaders guiding by Our command. And We inspired to them the doing of good deeds, the establishment of prayer, and the giving of zakah; and they were worshippers of Us.﴾

[Surah Anbiyā' 21:73]

A role model must be complete and the Prophets must be infallible; this is what logic entails and the Sacred Law necessitates. We will shed light on this in another work, God-willing, to refute some of the unclear issues about the infallibility of Prophets عليهم السلام, to clarify the truth and to spread its light. And God is our Guardian and what an excellent Trustee is He!

Chapter Three

Seemingly Unclear Matters about the Infallibility of Prophets عليهم السلام and their Invalidating Responses

Someone could object saying, "How can Prophets be infallible while we know that the Quran has established that some have committed some infractions, and others from amongst them have sins and blatant disobedience attributed to them?"

It was said about Prophet Adam عليه السلام:

﴿ وَعَصَىٰ آدَمُ رَبَّهُ فَغَوَىٰ ﴾

﴿*And Adam 'disobeyed' his Lord and erred.*﴾

[Surah Ṭāhā 20:121]

And it was said about Prophet Nuh عليه السلام:

﴿ إِنِّي أَعِظُكَ أَن تَكُونَ مِنَ الْجَاهِلِينَ ﴾

﴿*Indeed, I advise you, lest you be among the ignorant.* ﴾

[Surah Hud 11:46]

And it was said about the Master of the Messengers ﷺ:

﴿ لِيَغْفِرَ لَكَ اللَّهُ مَا تَقَدَّمَ مِن ذَنبِكَ وَمَا تَأَخَّرَ.. ﴾

﴿*That Allah may forgive for you what preceded of your sin and what will follow.*﴾

[Surah Fatḥ 48:2]

To answer the above, we say: The infallibility of Prophets is proven by the texts of the Quran and will be understood by anyone with sound reason and who is rooted in knowledge since how could it be conceivable that Allah ﷻ could command humanity to follow them, emulate them, and follow their footsteps, if they were not examples of human perfection, exemplars for virtue, nobility, and purity! And were infallibility not part of their attributes, we would not be responsible for following them in all of their works and deeds!

As for what has been recorded in some texts of Sacred Law which may outwardly suggest that some Prophets ﷺ fell into disobedience and breaches, they are understood in the following light:

1. They were not acts of disobedience, but rather it was only acting contrary to the best course of action (*khilāf al-awlā*).

2. They were not acts of disobedience; it was only a minor mistake in judgment (*khaṭa'a fi 'l-ijtihād*).

3. Even if it were to be hypothetically accepted that they were infractions and acts of disobedience, then still they would have occurred prior to Prophethood.

We say this because it is not likely that Allah would lavish such praise on them if they were steeped in foul and repulsive deeds. We read that Allah Most High declares about them:

﴿أُولَئِكَ الَّذِينَ هَدَى اللَّهُ فَبِهُدَاهُمُ اقْتَدِهِ قُلْ لَا أَسْأَلُكُمْ عَلَيْهِ أَجْرًا إِنْ هُوَ إِلَّا ذِكْرَى لِلْعَالَمِينَ﴾

﴿*Those are the ones whom Allah has guided, so from their guidance take an example. Say, "I ask of you for this message no payment. It is not but a reminder for the worlds."*﴾

[Surah An'ām 6:90]

Meaning: 'Follow them, O Muhammad, in their excellent conduct, their pure character, their chastity, their piety and righteousness."

Allah Most High says:

﴿وَجَعَلْنَاهُمْ أَئِمَّةً يَهْدُونَ بِأَمْرِنَا وَأَوْحَيْنَا إِلَيْهِمْ فِعْلَ الْخَيْرَاتِ وَإِقَامَ الصَّلَاةِ وَإِيتَاءَ الزَّكَاةِ ۖ وَكَانُوا لَنَا عَابِدِينَ﴾

﴿*And We made them leaders guiding by Our command. And We inspired to them the doing of good deeds, establishment of prayer, and giving of zakah; and they were worshippers of Us.*﴾

[Surah Anbiyā' 21:73]

Chapter Four

The Ostensible Disobedience of Prophet Adam ﷺ

The apparent disobedience of Prophet Adam ﷺ can be misunderstood from Allah's word in the Quran:

﴿ فَأَكَلَا مِنْهَا فَبَدَتْ لَهُمَا سَوْآتُهُمَا وَطَفِقَا يَخْصِفَانِ عَلَيْهِمَا مِن وَرَقِ الْجَنَّةِ ۚ وَعَصَىٰ
آدَمُ رَبَّهُ فَغَوَىٰ عَلَيْهِمَا مِن وَرَقِ الْجَنَّةِ ۚ وَعَصَىٰ آدَمُ رَبَّهُ فَغَوَىٰ ثُمَّ اجْتَبَاهُ رَبُّهُ فَتَابَ
عَلَيْهِ وَهَدَىٰ ﴾

﴿And Adam and his wife ate of it, and their private parts became apparent to them, and they began to fasten over themselves from the leaves of Paradise. And Adam disobeyed his Lord and erred. Then his Lord chose him and turned to him in forgiveness and guided [him].﴾

[Surah Ṭāhā 20:121-122]

This contravention and disobedience was only before Prophethood as proven by Allah Most High's Word:

﴿ ثُمَّ اجْتَبَاهُ رَبُّهُ ﴾

﴿Then his Lord selected him.﴾

His '*selection*' means Allah electing him for carrying His Message. Thus, the disobedience occurred from Adam ﷺ before Prophethood.

There is another opinion that Adam ﷺ only ate from the tree out of forgetfulness proven by Allah Most High's Word:

﴿ وَلَقَدْ عَهِدْنَا إِلَىٰ آدَمَ مِن قَبْلُ فَنَسِيَ وَلَمْ نَجِدْ لَهُ عَزْمًا ﴾

﴿And We had already taken a promise from Adam before, but he forgot; and We found not in him determination.﴾

[Surah Ṭāhā 20:115]

It is said that when Adam ﷺ was prohibited from eating from the forbidden tree by the following statement of Allah Most High:

﴿ وَلَا تَقْرَبَا هَـٰذِهِ الشَّجَرَةَ ﴾

﴿...do not approach this tree...﴾

[Surah Baqara 2:35]

Prophet Adam ﷺ understood that Allah was referring to *that specific tree* not its particular species, so he ate from another tree from the same species of tree, thus [inadvertently] contravening the command of Allah. That was him exercising his judgment from his side, not intentionally plotting and planning to contravene Allah's command.

The most acceptable opinion about this is that we say:

Adam ﷺ ate from the tree out of forgetfulness, and forgetfulness removes the liability of sin from the perpetrator, like the Messenger of Allah ﷺ said: '*My nation is absolved from mistakes, forgetfulness, and the evil deeds that they are forced to carry out.*' Allah indicates this notion:

﴿ رَبَّنَا لَا تُؤَاخِذْنَا إِن نَّسِينَا أَوْ أَخْطَأْنَا ﴾

﴿Our Lord, do not impose blame upon us if we have forgotten or erred.﴾

[Surah Baqara 2:286]

Adam ﷺ did not intentionally resolve to commit disobedience proven by the verse that we cited:

﴿ فَنَسِيَ وَلَمْ نَجِدْ لَهُ عَزْمًا ﴾

﴿...but he forgot; and We found not in him determination.﴾

[Surah Ṭāhā 20:115]

That is what scholars the likes of Imam al-Qurtubi ؒ and Ibn al-ʿArabī ؒ have concluded. Alternatively, we may say that disobedience can only occur *after* Prophethood [i.e. after they are tasked with prophethood], and that is what the author of *Tafsir al-Manār* opted for.

The following quote is mentioned in *Tafsir al-Manār*, in the first volume, on page 380:

> As for the issue of the infallibility of Adam ﷺ, keeping in line with the way of the pious fore bears, we conclude that his 'disobedience' and 'repentance' are among the ambiguous aspects similar to the rest of what came in the story from what outwardly does not give one peace of mind. So it is upon us to say, indeed those apparent 'disobediences' originated from him *before* Prophethood was conferred upon him. Allah, Sublime is His affair, said:

﴿ فَنَسِيَ وَلَمْ نَجِدْ لَهُ عَزْمًا ﴾

﴿*...but he forgot; and We found not in him determination.*﴾

[Surah Ṭāhā 20:115]

Scholars are unanimous that he was divinely protected from contravening the commands of Allah after Prophethood. It is plausible that what transpired with Ādam was due to forgetfulness. But, solely because of the veneration given to the command of Allah, it was termed disobedience because deeds done forgetfully and inadvertently are among those things that do not invalidate infallibility.

As for Ibn al-ʿArabī, he has inclined to the first opinion and believes that the apparent violation of Ādam was caused by forgetfulness. The following has been transmitted in his '*Book of Rulings of the Quran*' (*Kitāb aḥkām al-Quran*), volume 3 on page 1249 regarding this:

> How much has been said that exonerates the Prophets from those acts which do not befit their rank and what the nescient have attributed to them—such as them falling into sin, intentionally inclining to it, and boldly committing sins out of defiance while knowing it to be wrong. No, by God—because even the average Muslim scrupulously avoids that, so how about the case of the Prophets? However, the Creator —Whose Decree and Pre-Eternal Judgment is carried out—decreed Ādam to commit a violation and he fell into it deliberately and forgetfully.

It is said about his deliberateness:

﴿ وَعَصَىٰ آدَمُ رَبَّهُ ﴾

﴿*And Adam disobeyed his Lord.*﴾

[Surah Ṭāhā 20:121]

But, it is said in his defence explaining his excuse:

﴿ وَلَقَدْ عَهِدْنَا إِلَىٰ آدَمَ مِن قَبْلُ فَنَسِيَ وَلَمْ نَجِدْ لَهُ عَزْمًا ﴾

﴿*And We had already taken a promise from Adam before, but he forgot; and We found not in him determination.*﴾

[Surah Ṭāhā 20:115]

It is equivalent to a man taking an oath that he will never enter a certain house. Later, he deliberately enters it while forgetting his oath, or mistakenly enters due to misinterpreting the oath, thus he will be considered both deliberate *and* forgetful. His deliberateness is not connected to his forgetfulness. In a similar parable, a master can say about his servant out of disdain and reprimand '*he disobeyed*,' and then turn to him with grace and kindness and say '*he forgot*' to remove any feelings of blame, shame, or ill-will from him.

Then Ibn al-ʿArabī ؒ continues saying:

> It is not permissible for anyone among us today to proclaim that (i.e. the disobedience of Ādam ؑ) except when we mention it during the course of reciting Allah's Word ﷻ, or the words of His Prophet ﷺ. As for someone initiating this topic from his own self, in that case, it is not even permissible for us to speak about our near-ancestors in that manner who are similar to us. So how about the case of our most noble, most ancient and greatest forefather, the first Prophet ؑ whom Allah pardoned, turned to him in repentance, and forgave?

ʿAllāmah Qurṭubī ؒ said:

> The scholars differ: how did Ādam ؑ eat from the tree while there was a threat attached to approaching the tree which is in Allah's Word ﷻ:
>
> ﴿ فَتَكُونَا مِنَ الظَّالِمِينَ ﴾
>
> ﴾*...lest you be among the wrongdoers.*﴿
>
> [Surah Baqara 2:35]

The scholars of Sufism said:

> They both ate from the tree without that which is implied against them because they [Ādam and Ḥawwā ؑ] did not interpret the prohibition to apply to all trees of that species.

It is also said: "They ate from it out of forgetfulness," which is the correct opinion because Allah Most High declared as much in His Mighty Book, definitively and conclusively when He said:

﴿ وَلَقَدْ عَهِدْنَا إِلَىٰ آدَمَ مِن قَبْلُ فَنَسِيَ وَلَمْ نَجِدْ لَهُ عَزْمًا ﴾

﴾*And We had already taken a promise from Adam before, but he forgot; and We found not in him determination.*﴿

[Surah Ṭāhā 20:115]

However, since the Prophets ؑ are inseparable from Divine preservation and spiritual alertness because of their abundant gnosis, their lofty status and what is not expected from other than them, Ādam's ؑ being neglectful in recalling the prohibition became, for him, an act of disobedience i.e. a violation of Allah's command.

Abu Umamah ﷺ said:

> If all of the forbearance shown by the Children of Adam since Allah created creation until the Day of Judgment was placed on one pan of the scale, and the forbearance of Adam ﷺ was placed in the other, the forbearance of Adam would outweigh them all. Allah Most High said:
>
> ﴿ وَلَمْ نَجِدْ لَهُۥ عَزْمًا ﴾
>
> ﴿*...and We found not in him determination.*﴾
>
> [Surah Ṭāhā 20:115]

Since it has been made clear to us from the words of the scholars and exegetes of the Quran that Adam ﷺ did not deliberately contravene the command of Allah, Sublime and Majestic is He. He only ate from the tree because of a misinterpretation in judgment or forgetting the command of Allah, Blessed and Exalted is He. His Lord rebuked him by expelling him from Paradise and sent him down to earth and that was because of a Pre-Eternal Divine Wisdom. Therefore, it is not permissible for us to accuse him of sin because what transpired from him did not occur except out of forgetfulness—not because he forgot good manners. Especially, after the Quran revealed with Allah Most High's Word:

﴿ ثُمَّ اجْتَبَاهُ رَبُّهُۥ فَتَابَ عَلَيْهِ وَهَدَىٰ ﴾

﴿*Then his Lord chose him and turned to him in forgiveness and guided [him]!*﴾

[Surah Ṭāhā 20:122]

Chapter Five

The Infallibility of Prophet Ibrahim عليه السلام

As for Prophet Ibrahim عليه السلام, the Intimate Friend of Allah, some ambiguous texts have been transmitted in the Book and the Sunna which might give the incorrect impression that the Prophets wer not infallible. However, this outward appearance is not the intended meaning, because it stands in contradistinction to other definitive Quranic texts. So in such cases, there must be reconciliation between those texts to understand them in a way that is in accordance with the Muslim belief of the infallibility of the Noble Prophets عليهم السلام.

As for the first text:

﴿ فَلَمَّا جَنَّ عَلَيْهِ اللَّيْلُ رَأَى كَوْكَباً قَالَ هَـذَا رَبِّي فَلَمَّا أَفَلَ قَالَ لا أُحِبُّ الآفِلِينَ
فَلَمَّا رَأَى الْقَمَرَ بَازِغاً قَالَ هَـذَا رَبِّي فَلَمَّا أَفَلَ قَالَ لَئِن لَّمْ يَهْدِنِي رَبِّي لأَكُونَنَّ مِنَ
الْقَوْمِ الضَّالِّينَ   فَلَمَّا رَأَى الشَّمْسَ بَازِغَةً قَالَ هَـذَا رَبِّي هَـذَا أَكْبَرُ فَلَمَّا أَفَلَتْ قَالَ
يَا قَوْمِ إِنِّي بَرِيءٌ مِّمَّا تُشْرِكُونَ   إِنِّي وَجَّهْتُ وَجْهِيَ لِلَّذِي فَطَرَ السَّمَاوَاتِ وَالأَرْضَ
حَنِيفاً وَمَا أَنَاْ مِنَ الْمُشْرِكِينَ ﴾

﴾ So when the night covered him [with darkness], he saw a star. He said, "This is my lord." But when it set, he said, "I like not those that disappear. And when he saw the moon rising, he said, "This is my lord." But when it set, he said, "Unless my Lord guides me, I will surely be among the people gone astray. And when he saw the sun rising, he said, "This is my lord; this is greater." But when it set, he said, "O my people, indeed I am free from what you associate with Allah. Indeed, I have turned my face toward He who created the heavens and the earth, inclining toward truth, and I am not of those who associate others with Allah."﴿

[Surah Anʿām 6:76-79]

These verses may outwardly give the impression that Ibrahim عليه السلام harboured doubt about Allah, was ignorant about His Greatness, and was unaware who exactly the true God was that deserved to be worshipped!

Some people might presume that Ibrahim عليه السلام was influenced by the environment of his people and in the beginning of his childhood, he worshipped the stars along with them just as they worshipped the sun and moon; this is blatant ignorance and just plain wrong. This would not emanate from anyone except one who was ignorant of the traits of the Noble Prophets عليهم السلام,[10] and one who did not understand the meanings of the wise Quran.

So Allah—How Sublime is His Praise—has proclaimed about His Prophet and His Intimate Friend, Ibrahim عليه السلام, that He caused him to gain awareness of the Kingdom of the heavens and earth, and that he was amongst the monotheistic believers, and among the perfected in faith and certainty. Also that Allah had gifted him complete guidance since his childhood and granted him عليه السلام an invalidating proof which broke the back of every stubborn and arrogant opponent.

He had an unparalleled talent for debate and furnishing proof of the existence of the One God that no one could defeat. Listen attentively to the core message of the following verse, how Allah provides proofs to 'the perfection of certainty,' Prophet Ibrahim عليه السلام, when He says:

﴿وَإِذْ قَالَ إِبْرَاهِيمُ لِأَبِيهِ آزَرَ أَتَتَّخِذُ أَصْنَامًا آلِهَةً إِنِّي أَرَاكَ وَقَوْمَكَ فِي ضَلَالٍ مُّبِينٍ. وَكَذَٰلِكَ نُرِي إِبْرَاهِيمَ مَلَكُوتَ السَّمَاوَاتِ وَالْأَرْضِ وَلِيَكُونَ مِنَ الْمُوقِنِينَ. فَلَمَّا جَنَّ عَلَيْهِ اللَّيْلُ رَأَىٰ كَوْكَبًا﴾...

﴿*And [mention, O Muhammad], when Ibrahim said to his father Azar, "Do you take idols as deities? Indeed, I see you and your people to be in manifest error. And thus did We show Ibrahim the realm of the heavens and the earth that he would be among the certain [in faith] So when the night covered him [with darkness], he saw a star."*﴾

[Surah An'ām 6:74-76]

So Allah granted Prophet Ibrahim عليه السلام convincing proofs and clear evidences which through them, established the proof of the existence of the Wise Designer, Allah. So he debated with his paternal uncle with his words:

﴿أَتَتَّخِذُ أَصْنَامًا آلِهَةً﴾

﴿*Do you take idols as deities?*﴾

[Surah 'An'ām 6:74]

[10] See footnote about traits of the Prophets on page 18

Thereafter, he ascribes his paternal uncle and his people with misguidance in their worship of what does not hear, nor see, and cannot help its worshipper in the least. So Allah said through the words of Ibrahim:

﴿إِنِّي أَرَاكَ وَقَوْمَكَ فِي ضَلَالٍ مُّبِينٍ﴾

﴿*Indeed, I see you and your people to be in manifest error.*﴾

[Surah Anʿām 6:74]

Then, proofs came to the 'perfection of certainty,' Ibrahim, m the endorsement of Allah, Exalted and Sublime is He:

﴿وَكَذَٰلِكَ نُرِي إِبْرَاهِيمَ مَلَكُوتَ السَّمَاوَاتِ وَالْأَرْضِ وَلِيَكُونَ مِنَ الْمُوقِنِينَ﴾

﴿*And thus did We show Abraham the realm of the heavens and the earth that he would be among the certain [in faith].*﴾

[Surah Anʿām 6:75]

The verses that follow are nothing other than Prophet Ibrahim establishing proofs for the existence of God and establishing a proof against his people in a way that comes down to their level of comprehension and understanding—and it came down to their level according to what *they believed*. He said about the star: '*This is my Lord*,' and said the same about the moon and the sun as a strategy to eventually invalidate their beliefs about worshipping these supposed 'gods' with sound logic, proofs, and evidences. For this reason, Allah concluded this story with His Word:

﴿وَتِلْكَ حُجَّتُنَا آتَيْنَاهَا إِبْرَاهِيمَ عَلَىٰ قَوْمِهِ ۚ نَرْفَعُ دَرَجَاتٍ مَّن نَّشَاءُ ۗ
إِنَّ رَبَّكَ حَكِيمٌ عَلِيمٌ﴾

﴿*And that was Our [conclusive] argument which We gave Ibrahim against his people. We raise by degrees whom We will. Indeed, your Lord is Wise and Knowing.*﴾

[Surah Anʿām 6:83]

ʿAllāmah al-Zamakhsharī mentioned a very satisfying passage which contains the utmost generosity and precision. We will quote some of it about the *tafsir* of this verse here. He says:

> His father and his people used to worship idols, the sun, the moon and the stars. So he wanted to alert them to the error in their way of life, and to guide them to the way of contemplation and rational proofs. And to make them recognize that the correct perspective is

> that none of those things would be eligible of being a god by erecting the proof of contingency in them, and that behind those things, is a 'Causer' which caused them to be, and a 'Designer' which designed them, and a 'Planner' which manages their rising and setting, their moving and their routes, and the rest of their states.
>
> The words of Ibrahim عليه السلام ﴾*...this is my Lord...*﴿ is the word of someone [temporarily] giving credence to his opponent while knowing that the opponent is wrong. So he عليه السلام relates his opponent's position exactly as he stated it, without being overzealous to his own position, because this strategy will attract his opponent to the truth, and is more peaceful than quarrelling.
>
> Thereafter, he refutes it after re-stating it to invalidate it by proof when he said, ﴾*I do not love things that vanish*﴿ i.e. I do not love the worship of gods who change from one state to another, move from one place to another, and who can be covered by veils, because that is amongst the attributes of temporal bodies [and God is unlike temporal bodies].
>
> And his عليه السلام word, ﴾*unless my Lord guides me, I will surely be among the people gone astray*﴿ [Surah 'An'ām 6:77] is a warning to his people that whomsoever takes the moon as a god – since it disappears like all celestial bodies – is misguided. And guidance to the truth comes solely from Allah's Divine Grace (*tawfīq*) and His Gentleness.

So the story that the Quran depicts is nothing other than an archetype to the ways of persuasion and the power of proof which Allah ﷻ granted to His Prophet and His Intimate Friend, Ibrahim عليه السلام, and how he was able to cause his people to understand by establishing proofs for the existence of God, and that he proved to them their misguidance and their error in worshipping the celestial bodies—the sun and the moon. It became clear that Ibrahim عليه السلام had taken the easiest of paths with them to arrive at his goal. He did not directly confront them about misguidance, rather he took a gradual, step-by-step approach with them.

So first he claimed that the stars he saw shining in the sky were his Lord so that they would feel comfortable with what he was saying. Then, when the stars were no longer visible, Ibrahim عليه السلام rejected the idea that these stars were fit to be the Lord because they change and are transitory, and that is the sign of contingency.

Then, when he saw the moon shining prominently in the sky, he said ﴾*this is my Lord*﴿. When the moon set and its light disappeared, he rejected that it could be the worshipped Lord. Here, Ibrahim عليه السلام alluded to their misguidance, however, in a way displaying the pinnacle of wisdom, when he said:

﴿ لَئِن لَّمْ يَهْدِنِي رَبِّي لَأَكُونَنَّ مِنَ الْقَوْمِ الضَّالِّينَ ﴾

﴿*Unless my Lord guides me, I will surely be among the people gone astray.*﴾

[Surah An'ām 6:77]

So take note here, he did not explicitly point out their misguidance. Instead, he merely accused himself of misguidance if he was to worship this transient, ephemeral god that manifested the signs of contingency to him. And his words ﴿*...among the people gone astray*﴾ alludes to the misguidance of whoever worships the moon.

Then, when the sun rose and its golden rays shone upon the earth and illuminated the world he ﷺ said, 'This sun is my Lord, because it is the largest creation and it has more of a right to be worshipped than the rest of the stars and celestial bodies.' He said this [to strategically agree with their premise] to later establish a proof *against* their misguidance. But when the sun set and it disappeared below the horizon, and it did not produce any light or radiance, it was only at this point that he explicitly mentioned the misguidance of whosoever worships it—or anything else that is contingent, and he absolved himself from his community and from their worship of it and that was after the proof became crystal clear, the truth had dawned, and the objective was clearly achieved.

﴿ قَالَ يَا قَوْمِ إِنِّي بَرِيءٌ مِّمَّا تُشْرِكُونَ ﴿٧٨﴾ إِنِّي وَجَّهْتُ وَجْهِيَ لِلَّذِي فَطَرَ السَّمَاوَاتِ وَالْأَرْضَ حَنِيفًا وَمَا أَنَا مِنَ الْمُشْرِكِينَ ﴿٧٩﴾ وَحَاجَّهُ قَوْمُهُ قَالَ أَتُحَاجُّونِّي فِي اللَّهِ وَقَدْ هَدَانِ وَلَا أَخَافُ مَا تُشْرِكُونَ بِهِ إِلَّا أَن يَشَاءَ رَبِّي شَيْئًا وَسِعَ رَبِّي كُلَّ شَيْءٍ عِلْمًا أَفَلَا تَتَذَكَّرُونَ ﴿٨٠﴾ وَكَيْفَ أَخَافُ مَا أَشْرَكْتُمْ وَلَا تَخَافُونَ أَنَّكُمْ أَشْرَكْتُم بِاللَّهِ مَا لَمْ يُنَزِّلْ بِهِ عَلَيْكُمْ سُلْطَانًا فَأَيُّ الْفَرِيقَيْنِ أَحَقُّ بِالْأَمْنِ إِن كُنتُمْ تَعْلَمُونَ ﴿٨١﴾ الَّذِينَ آمَنُوا وَلَمْ يَلْبِسُوا إِيمَانَهُم بِظُلْمٍ أُولَٰئِكَ لَهُمُ الْأَمْنُ وَهُم مُّهْتَدُونَ ﴿٨٢﴾ وَتِلْكَ حُجَّتُنَا آتَيْنَاهَا إِبْرَاهِيمَ عَلَىٰ قَوْمِهِ نَرْفَعُ دَرَجَاتٍ مَّن نَّشَاءُ إِنَّ رَبَّكَ حَكِيمٌ عَلِيمٌ ﴾

﴿*...O my people, indeed I am free from what you associate with Allah. Indeed, I have turned my face toward He who created the heavens and the earth, inclining toward truth, and I am not of those who associate others with Allah. And his people argued with him. He said, "Do you argue with me concerning Allah while He has guided me? And I fear not what you associate with Him [and will not be harmed] unless my Lord should will something.*

My Lord encompasses all things in knowledge; then will you not remember? And how should I fear what you associate while you do not fear that you have associated with Allah that for which He has not sent down to you any authority? So which of the two parties has more right to security, if you should know? They who believe and do not mix their belief with injustice - those will have security, and they are [rightly] guided. And that was Our [conclusive] argument which We gave Abraham against his people. We raise by degrees whom We will. Indeed, your Lord is Wise and Knowing.﴾

[Surah Anʿām 6:78-83]

So it is clear that these statements of Ibrahim ﷺ, the Intimate Friend of Allah, were not out of harbouring doubt in Allah, nor were they out of ignorance of the Creator, Sublime and Lofty is He. It was merely from the most obvious ways of establishing the proof of his community's misguidance by way of proofs and evidences, and silencing them with the greatest irrefutable proofs.

Ibn al-ʿArabī ﷺ says in his *Tafsir aḥkām al-Quran*:

> The fact that Ibrahim ﷺ was given knowledge of debating by furnishing evidence *to prove monotheism*, this in itself proves the infallibility of Ibrahim ﷺ and exonerates him from being considered ignorant about Allah Most High and harbouring doubt about Him. It also clarifies that what happened between him ﷺ and his community was only to establish proofs [for them], not to show his beliefs.

Whosoever thinks that Ibrahim ﷺ harboured doubt about Allah or believes that he worshipped the sun or the stars, has missed the mark, has misunderstood, and is ignorant about the traits of the Prophets and Messengers ﷺ. How could that be possible while Allah, Sublime and Majestic is He, had granted him intelligence and perfect guidance *before Prophethood*:

﴿ وَلَقَدْ آتَيْنَا إِبْرَاهِيمَ رُشْدَهُ مِن قَبْلُ وَكُنَّا بِهِ عَالِمِينَ ﴾

﴿*And We had certainly given Abraham his sound judgement before, and We were of him well-Knowing.*﴾

[Surah Anbiyāʾ 21:51]

As for the second Quranic verse which could give the impression that Ibrahim ﷺ was not infallible is Allah Most High's Word:

﴿ وَإِذْ قَالَ إِبْرَاهِيمُ رَبِّ أَرِنِي كَيْفَ تُحْيِي الْمَوْتَىٰ قَالَ أَوَلَمْ تُؤْمِن قَالَ بَلَىٰ وَلَٰكِن لِّيَطْمَئِنَّ قَلْبِي قَالَ فَخُذْ أَرْبَعَةً مِّنَ الطَّيْرِ فَصُرْهُنَّ إِلَيْكَ ثُمَّ اجْعَلْ عَلَىٰ كُلِّ جَبَلٍ

مِّنْهُنَّ جُزْءًا ثُمَّ ادْعُهُنَّ يَأْتِينَكَ سَعْيًا ۚ وَاعْلَمْ أَنَّ اللَّهَ عَزِيزٌ حَكِيمٌ ﴾

﴿*And mention when Ibrahim said, "My Lord, show me how You give life to the dead." Allah said, "Have you not believed?" He said, "Yes, but I ask only that my heart may be satisfied." Allah said, "Take four birds and commit them to yourself. Then after slaughtering them put on each mountain a portion of them; then call them - they will come [jogging] to you in haste. And know that Allah is Exalted in Might and Wise."*﴾

[Surah Baqara 2:260]

This sacred text could be misinterpreted to mean that Ibrahim ﷺ, the Intimate Friend of Allah, doubted the Power of Allah to give life to the dead, and that would be an incorrect understanding. God forbid that Ibrahim ﷺ harboured doubts about his Lord or about Allah Most High's Power while being the patriarch of the Prophets (*Abu 'l-'Anbiyā'*) who laid the foundations of monotheism, and re-built the first House for the worship of Allah, the One, the Sustainer. Accordingly, Ibrahim ﷺ only asked about 'how' meaning ﴿*how do you give life to the dead?*﴾ and he did not ask about the essence of resurrection. Thus, he did not say, "Are You capable, O Lord, of giving life to the dead?" The question about 'how' is only out of longing and wanting to be shown the secrets of Divine-creating.

Shaykh Ahmad al-Munīr ﷺ says the following in his footnotes on *Tafsir al-Kashshāf*:

> As for the question of the Intimate Friend ﷺ ﴿*how do you give life to the dead?*﴾, this was not out of doubt in the Power of Allah to give life – God forbid. Rather, this is a question of '*how*' do you give life? It is not a prerequisite of faith to encompass *how* a thing happens, but rather it was only a request for knowledge which was not essential to *faith*. This is indicated by the question '*how*' and that is a question regarding the state. This question is equivalent to someone saying: 'How does Zaid judge between people?' The questioner does not doubt that Zaid rules people, rather he asks about '*how he judges*' not if he is established as a judge.

If misgivings bother the minds of some people in thinking that Ibrahim ﷺ harboured doubt about Allah from these verses, then the Prophet Muhammad ﷺ severed the root of this problem with his words:

"*We have more propensity to doubt than Ibrahim* ﷺ," i.e. since we do not doubt, therefore, it is more befitting and more believable that Ibrahim ﷺ did not either.

Allah intended by His Words ﴿*have you not believed?*﴾ [Surah Baqara

2:260] to cause Ibrahim ﷺ to articulate: ﴾*Of course [I have believed]*﴿ to remove any negative implications that the prior statement may give rise to, and for his belief to remain untainted. He was quoted using the Arabic word ﴾*balā*﴿ meaning ﴾*of course!*﴿ which would be clearly understood by everyone who hears it and no one could doubt him about it.

Sayyid Qutub said in his *Tafsir, In the Shade of the Quran,* about this verse that is quoted below:

﴿ وَإِذْ قَالَ إِبْرَاهِيمُ رَبِّ أَرِنِي كَيْفَ تُحْيِي الْمَوْتَى ﴾

﴾*And mention when Abraham said, "My Lord, show me how You give life to the dead."*﴿

[Surah Baqara 2:260]

Ibrahim ﷺ wanted to observe the hidden secret of Godly creation. So when the desire to observe this came to Ibrahim ﷺ—the penitent, forbearing, the firm believer, the one pleased with His Lord, the devout, the worshipful, the proximate, the Intimate Friend—it uncovered what occasionally stirs in one's heart from yearning and seeking to observe the secrets of Godly creation in the hearts of the closest of those brought-nigh!

This 'desire to observe' is not a question of whether or not Prophet Ibrahim ﷺ possessed belief, whether it was firmly established in him, or even about its perfection. But neither was he seeking a proof, nor attempting to 'strengthen his faith.' It is actually something completely different. It is a completely different experience. It is the soul's yearning to observe the veiled secret of God in a practical circumstance. To experience the re-making of a human being is a completely different experience than merely believing in the unseen. Since he—Prophet Ibrahim ﷺ, the Intimate Friend of Allah—spoke to his Lord and his Lord spoke to him—then there can be no faith beyond that level nor a greater proof needed for faith. However, he wanted to observe the Hand of God (i.e. the Power of God) in action—to obtain this special experience of bringing the dead back to life—to witness God's handiwork, to breathe in its air, and to live the experience. He possessed a completely different level of *īmān* than the type of *īmān* which has the potential for adding more *īmān* to it! Nay, this is of the highest echelons of *īmān* possessed by the Khalil—Prophet Ibrahim ﷺ.

What were the Three Equivocations (Lies) of Ibrahim ﷺ?

As for what was transmitted in the Prophetic *Sunna* that ostensibly alludes to the absence of infallibility regarding Ibrahim ﷺ, it is reflected in the words of the Prophet ﷺ:

> Ibrahim ﷺ did not lie except three 'lies.' Two of them between him and his people, namely, 1) his word ❮Indeed, I am sick❯[11] and 2) his word ❮Rather, the biggest of them did it❯.[12] The third is in reference to what the Prophet ﷺ stated, 'One day, he [Ibrahim] and Sarah came upon a tyrant [Nimrod] from among tyrants. It was said to [the tyrant]: 'Certainly, there is a man and a woman from the best of people.' So the tyrant sent someone to Ibrahim ﷺ and asked about her: 'Who is she?' He said: 'my sister.'

> 'So Ibrahim ﷺ went and said to her: 'Truly, if this tyrant comes to know you are my wife, he will overpower me and take you. So if he asks you, then tell him you are my sister.... because you are my sister in Islam and there are no believers on the face of the earth other than me and you.'

> 'So the tyrant sent for her and she was brought. Then Ibrahim ﷺ stood up and began praying the ritual prayer. When she came to the tyrant, he went to grab her with his hand. Suddenly, he became paralyzed until his feet began to tremble. He said: 'Pray to Allah for me and I will not hurt you.' So she prayed to Allah and he released her. Then, he tried to grab her a second time but was seized like before or even more severely. So he said: 'Pray to Allah for me and I will not hurt you. So she prayed to Allah and he decided to release her from his custody. So he summoned some of his chamberlains and said: 'You did not bring me a human, you only brought me a devil!' Hajar was given to provide services for Sarah. She [Sarah] came to Ibrahim ﷺ while he was standing and performing the ritual prayer and he gestured with his hand. She said: "Allah has repulsed the plot of the disbeliever back down his throat. So I was given Hajar to provide services.' Abu Hurairah ؓ said: "That is your mother, O Arabs (lit. O Children of water from the sky)." (Bukhari and Muslim)

This *hadith* does not contain anything that would indicate the absence of infallibility of Ibrahim ﷺ because the Prophet Muhammad ﷺ did not intend, by these three equivocations, the true meaning of a lie. He ﷺ only intended that Ibrahim ﷺ, the Intimate Friend of Allah, made [ambiguous] statements that could be misunderstood to be a lie, while in reality they were not.

So Ibrahim's ﷺ statement to his community: ❮I am sick❯ and his statement: ❮Rather, the biggest of them did it; this one...❯ is a type of disdain and mockery of them and their gods which they worshipped. He intended a metaphorical meaning by his words ❮I am sick❯, i.e. I am sick of your worshipping these idols that can neither hear, nor benefit, nor enrich their devotees in the least. So just like a human can be physical-

---

[11] Quran 37:89 (Saffat)
[12] Quran 21:63 (Anbiya')

ly sick, so too can he be spiritually sick. Especially if he sees his community lost in ignorance and misguidance while he is inviting them to guidance. However, they were lost in the fog of their misguidance, wandering aimlessly!

His words ﴾*Rather, their biggest one did it; this one...*﴿ was not in reality a lie. It was only presenting a type of irrefutable evidence against their argument and a clear proof that Ibrahim ﷺ wanted to establish against his community. So when they asked him who destroyed these idols, he pointed to the biggest, mute idol, to deride them and those idols. Then, when he saw them dumbfounded at his speech, he retorted with a silencing response ﴾*...so ask them if they can speak.*﴿.

As for his words to his wife Sarah '*you are my sister,*' he simply intended *my sister in creed* (*ʿaqīda*) and *my sister in īmān,* as Allah Most High declared:

﴿ إِنَّمَا الْمُؤْمِنُونَ إِخْوَةٌ ﴾

﴾*The believers are but a fraternity.*﴿

[Surah Ḥujurāt 49:10]

He did not intend a blood sister by that statement because she was his wife and not his blood sister. That was just an insinuation and not a lie whereby one perpetrating such a lie can be rebuked for and earn sin. For the Messenger Allah ﷺ said: '*There is a type of insinuation that is not considered to be lying*' i.e. an insinuation which does not cause a Muslim to fall into a lie. Thus, in the speech of Ibrahim ﷺ there is not the smallest jot that indicates to intentional lying which would detract from the infallibility of Prophet Ibrahim ﷺ, rather merely a type of permissible insinuation. Indeed, Allah speaks the truth and He guides to the right path.

Chapter Six

The Infallibility of Prophet Yusuf (عليه السلام)

The story that the Quran depicts to us of the veracious Yusuf (عليه السلام) contains several glimpses into the impeccable nature of this Noble Prophet (عليه السلام), his exoneration, and his infallibility. It mentions that Allah clad him with striking beauty, magnificence, and majesty, to the extent that he was tempted by the wife of the royal minister – i.e. the minister of Egypt. So she did whatever she did to seduce and trick him. However, he (عليه السلام) was tougher than steel and stronger than the mountains, hence the raging winds of lust which the women concocted, along with the wife of the minister, did not stir in him. The Quran relates to us a portion of the incident as Allah Most High said:

﴿وَقَالَ نِسْوَةٌ فِي الْمَدِينَةِ امْرَأَتُ الْعَزِيزِ تُرَاوِدُ فَتَاهَا عَن نَّفْسِهِ ۖ قَدْ شَغَفَهَا حُبًّا ۖ إِنَّا
لَنَرَاهَا فِي ضَلَالٍ مُّبِينٍ فَلَمَّا سَمِعَتْ بِمَكْرِهِنَّ أَرْسَلَتْ إِلَيْهِنَّ وَأَعْتَدَتْ لَهُنَّ مُتَّكَأً
وَآتَتْ كُلَّ وَاحِدَةٍ مِّنْهُنَّ سِكِّينًا وَقَالَتِ اخْرُجْ عَلَيْهِنَّ ۖ فَلَمَّا رَأَيْنَهُ أَكْبَرْنَهُ وَقَطَّعْنَ
أَيْدِيَهُنَّ وَقُلْنَ حَاشَ لِلَّهِ مَا هَٰذَا بَشَرًا إِنْ هَٰذَا إِلَّا مَلَكٌ كَرِيمٌ﴾

﴾And women in the city said, "The wife of the minister is seeking to seduce her slave boy; he has impassioned her with love. Indeed, we see her to be in clear error." So when she heard of their scheming, she sent for them and prepared for them a banquet and gave each one of them a knife and said [to Joseph], "Come out before them." And when they saw him, they greatly admired him and cut their hands and said, "Perfect is Allah! This is not a man; this is none but a noble angel."﴿

[Surah Yusuf 12:30-31]

Fabrication and Slander

One of the things that is worth noting is that some of the nescient and simple-minded, who do not have a firm-footing in knowledge, have allowed themselves to be deceived by some untrue, incorrect Judaeo-Christian reports (*Isrā'īlīyāt*) which are not valid to narrate or to be mentioned in the books of *tafsir*. The reliable scholars and the trustworthy *hadith* masters have warned us about them because they contradict the texts of the Quran and they contradict the concept of infallibility of the pure Prophets عليهم السلام.

Among these fabricated narrations about the veracious Yusuf عليه السلام is that when the wife of the minister attempted to seduce him and entice him to have relations with her, he responded to her, stayed in the quarters with her, and tried to commit the indecent act with her. He عليه السلام untied his trousers, lowered himself between her four appendages, and was on the verge of beginning the indecent act while she was lying flat on her back (lit. on the nape of her neck). However, he عليه السلام heard a voice calling him and saw his father (Yaqub عليه السلام) biting his fingers; it was shown to him on the wall of the chamber. So he became embarrassed and shy and abandoned the indecent act that he was interested in doing with the wife of the minister.

Those people who believe this myth forgot that the ever-truthful Yusuf عليه السلام is an honoured Prophet and Allah had divinely protected and fortified him from the spiritual filth of disobedience and obscenities. And which evil deed is more atrocious and a greater sign of obscenity than committing fornication? As if that accusation wasn't bad enough, they accuse him of betraying his master who made a covenant with him, raised him, treated him excellently, and provided him the best of abodes!

﴿ وَقَالَ الَّذِي اشْتَرَاهُ مِن مِّصْرَ لِامْرَأَتِهِ أَكْرِمِي مَثْوَاهُ عَسَىٰ أَن يَنفَعَنَا أَوْ نَتَّخِذَهُ وَلَدًا ۚ ﴾

﴿*And the one from Egypt who bought him said to his wife, "Make his residence comfortable. Perhaps he will benefit us, or we will adopt him as a son."*﴾

[Surah Yusuf 12:21]

The veracious Yusuf did not forget this beautiful treatment from his master. Rather, he actually pointed it out to the wife of the minister when she attempted to seduce him. With all of the beautiful treatment and excellence his master showed him, how could he ever betray his master regarding his wife?

Allah's Word ﴿*He said, "I seek the refuge of Allah. Indeed, he is my liege-lord*﴾ i.e. my master and in charge of my affairs ﴿*who has made good my residence. Indeed, wrongdoers will not succeed."*﴾ [Surah Yusuf 12:23]

Truly, fornication is one of the most repugnant crimes; all heavenly religions prohibit it. So how could a Prophet amongst Allah's Prophets commit it? Transcendent are You, Allah! This is a great slander indeed.

The reason those people proceeded hastily into accepting the likes of these untrue lies is relying upon Judaeo-Christian reports (*Isrā'illīyāt*) and misunderstanding the text of the Quran. What those simple-minded people understood is incorrect and does not agree with the infallibility of Prophets and is not in harmony with other Quranic texts.

That verse is Allah's Word:

﴿ وَلَقَدْ هَمَّتْ بِهِ وَهَمَّ بِهَا لَوْلَا أَنْ رَأَى بُرْهَانَ رَبِّهِ ﴾

﴾*And she certainly determined [to seduce] him, and he would have inclined to her had he not seen the proof of his Lord.*﴿

[Surah Yusuf 12:24]

The Incorrect Interpretation

Some scholars have explained 'concern' (*hamm*) from Yusuf to mean that he acceded to the wife of the minister and resolved to approach her. They explained the *proof* in the above verse to mean that an image of his father Yaqub biting his fingertips was seen by him, and then Yusuf abandoned the repugnant act.

This interpretation is absolutely false and impermissible to transmit under any circumstance, because it is a proven Judaeo-Christian report. Many of the exegetes (*mufassirīn*) have brought attention to the likes of these Judaeo-Christian reports and clarified its falsehood so that Muslims are not deceived by them, and are not led to believe that these reports are true.

The Correct Interpretation

ʿAllamah, Shaykh ʿAbdullah b. Aḥmad al-Nasafi in his *Tafsir* states:

> The words of Allah ﴾*...when she was interested in him*﴿ means she was interested *and determined* to do evil with him and ﴾*he was interested in her*﴿ means he had a natural human interest yet restrained himself. And if his interest was like her interest, Allah Most High would not have praised him saying that he was among His chosen slaves.

Some scholars explained the proof to be that: '*he heard a voice calling him saying: 'Beware! Beware of her!' twice. Then he heard in the third: 'Turn away from her!' but it did not benefit him, until Yaqub appeared to him biting his fingertips*' to the end of the report.

Shaykh al-Nasafi ؒ said:

All of the above claims are incorrect; Yusuf's own words indicate to the untruth of her claim of his advances:

﴿ نَفْسِي عَنْ رَاوَدَتْنِي هِيَ ﴾

﴾ *[Joseph] said, "It was she who sought to seduce me."* ﴿

[Surah Yusuf 12:23].

And if her allegation was true, he would not absolve himself from that.

And when he ؑ said in the Quran:

﴿ ذَٰلِكَ لِيَعْلَمَ أَنِّي لَمْ أَخُنْهُ بِالْغَيْبِ ﴾

﴾ *That is so the minister will know that I did not betray him in [his] absence...* ﴿

[Surah Yusuf 12:53]

Were the claims to be true, he would have betrayed his master.

Allah mentions:

﴿ كَذَٰلِكَ لِنَصْرِفَ عَنْهُ السُّوءَ وَالْفَحْشَاءَ ﴾

﴾ *And thus it was that We should avert from him evil and immorality* ﴿

[Surah Yusuf 12:24]

And if he did perpetrate the act, then evil would not have been averted from him ؑ.

I say: This verse contains a subtle meaning that no person of knowledge and insight be heedless of it.

That is because the *interest* which befell the wife of the minister was sinful. She invited him to commit the act of indecency. So to that end, she attempted to seduce him after meticulously locking all the doors and entrapping him in the chamber, as Allah Most High said:

﴿ وَرَاوَدَتْهُ الَّتِي هُوَ فِي بَيْتِهَا عَن نَّفْسِهِ وَغَلَّقَتِ الْأَبْوَابَ وَقَالَتْ هَيْتَ لَكَ ۚ قَالَ مَعَاذَ اللَّهِ ۖ إِنَّهُ رَبِّي أَحْسَنَ مَثْوَايَ ۖ إِنَّهُ لَا يُفْلِحُ الظَّالِمُونَ ﴾

﴾ *And she, in whose house he was, sought to seduce him. She closed the doors* and said, "Come, you." He said, "[I seek] the refuge of Allah. Indeed, he is my master, who has made good my residence. Indeed, wrongdoers will not succeed."⟩

[Surah Yusuf 12:23]

As for the *'interest'* that was from the veracious Yusuf, it was not an evil interest. Nor was he resolved to betray his master or commit indecency with his wife. Nor did the most miniscule thought of intending evil or acting indecently, which crosses the mind of some ignorant people, occur to Prophet Yusuf ﷺ. His *interest* was only to repel enmity from him, which would have come from his master, and to repel this filthy plot from him, which was concocted by the wife of the minister. For this reason, we find firmness and assertiveness in him in this scenario and harsh opposition in his speech:

﴿ قَالَ مَعَاذَ اللَّهِ ۖ إِنَّهُ رَبِّي أَحْسَنَ مَثْوَايَ ﴾

⟨ He said, "[I seek] the refuge of Allah. Indeed, he is my master, who has made good my residence."⟩

[Surah Yusuf 12:23]

Therefore, her *interest* is categorically different to his *interest*. She was interested in him in an evil way. He was interested in keeping her away, as some of the scholars of Quran have mentioned.

Or we say: Her *interest* was *her choice* and her own decision, whereas the *interest* of Yusuf was a natural human instinct and not his decision i.e. that he ﷺ inclined to her out of a primordial human response while restraining himself from succumbing to the sin. Human beings are not held accountable for what their souls desire or what their human natures incline towards, provided that they do not resolve to perform it.[13]

This is also what Imam al-Nasafi ؒ explained when he said: ⟨She was <u>interested</u> in him⟩ i.e. she resolved and desired to do evil and ⟨he was <u>interested</u> in her⟩, refers to his normal biological desire while restraining himself.

---

[13] In elucidating this, a rigorously authentic hadith states: "Verily Allah has recorded the good deeds and the evil deeds." Then he clarified that: "Whosoever intends to do a good deed but does not do it, Allah records it with Himself as a complete good deed; but if he intends it and does it, Allah records it with Himself as ten good deeds, up to seven hundred times, or more than that. But if he intends to do an evil deed and does not do it, Allah records it with Himself as a complete good deed; but if he intends it and does it, Allah records it down as one single evil deed." (Bukhari & Muslim)

Some of the scholars of *tafsir* opine that in the sequence is reversed in these (*taqdīm wa ta'khīr*) such that the meaning becomes: ﴾*If he did not see the proof of his Lord*﴿—and here the *proof of Allah* means the divine protection of Allah for Yusuf against his interest in her—*he would have committed the act*. However, the divine protection of Allah Most High for him *did* protect him.

Scholars of *tafsir* provide other explanations that acquit the Noble Yusuf ﵇ of the things that the People of the Book attribute to him, and of what some simple-minded Muslims have accepted from the apocryphal Judaeo-Christian reports.

Ten Proofs for the Infallibility of Prophet Yusuf ﵇

There are ten reasons of the infallibility of Yusuf ﵇ and his exoneration from the repugnant accusations that are ascribed to him. These are summarized below:

The First Proof

Prophet Yusuf's rejecting the unwanted advances from the minister's wife and the firm stance he took against her.

﴾ قَالَ مَعَاذَ اللَّهِ ۖ إِنَّهُ رَبِّي أَحْسَنَ مَثْوَايَ ۖ إِنَّهُ لَا يُفْلِحُ الظَّالِمُونَ ﴿

﴾*And she, in whose house he was, sought to seduce him. She closed the doors and said, "Come, you." He said, "[I seek] the refuge of Allah. Indeed, he is my master, who has made good my residence. Indeed, wrongdoers will not succeed."*﴿

[Surah Yusuf 12:23]

The Second Proof

Prophet Yusuf ﵇ fleeing from the wife of the minister, Zulaykha, after she entrapped him, tightened the proverbial noose, and intended to seduce him using force and compulsion. If Yusuf ﵇ was interested in committing indecency, he would not have fled from her, because the one who wants to commit indecency goes forward and does not retreat. Allah Most High declared:

﴿ وَاسْتَبَقَا الْبَابَ وَقَدَّتْ قَمِيصَهُ مِن دُبُرٍ وَأَلْفَيَا سَيِّدَهَا لَدَى الْبَابِ ﴾

﴿*And they both raced to the door, and she tore his shirt from the back, and they found her husband at the door*﴾

[Surah Yusuf 12:25]

The Third Proof

A relative of the minister's wife [an infant] testified to the innocence of Prophet Yusuf. The infant bid them to inspect his torn garment, because if he was advancing towards her while she was resisting, his shirt would have been ripped from the front. If, however, she was advancing towards him while he was resisting and fleeing from her, then his shirt would be ripped from behind. Allah said:

﴿ وَشَهِدَ شَاهِدٌ مِّنْ أَهْلِهَا إِن كَانَ قَمِيصُهُ قُدَّ مِن قُبُلٍ ﴾

﴿*And a witness from her family testified. "If his shirt is torn from the front,*﴾

i.e. and it was indeed torn from the front.

﴿ فَصَدَقَتْ وَهُوَ مِنَ الْكَاذِبِينَ وَإِنْ كَانَ قَمِيصُهُ قُدَّ مِن دُبُرٍ... ﴾

﴿*...then she has told the truth, and he is of the liars. But if his shirt is torn from the back...*﴾

i.e. it was not torn from the back.

﴿ فَكَذَبَتْ وَهُوَ مِنَ الصَّادِقِينَ فَلَمَّا رَأَى قَمِيصَهُ قُدَّ مِن دُبُرٍ قَالَ إِنَّهُ مِن كَيْدِكُنَّ إِنَّ كَيْدَكُنَّ عَظِيمٌ ﴾

﴿*...then she has lied, and he is of the truthful. So when her husband saw his shirt torn from the back, he said, "Indeed, it is of the women's plan. Indeed, your plan is great."*﴾

[Surah Yusuf 12:27-28]

It is said that the one who testified was an infant who was in the cradle, whom Allah caused to miraculously speak with this invalidating proof to manifest the exoneration of Yusuf ﷺ and he is one of three who spoke in the cradle. This is no surprise because Allah has Power over all things.

The Fourth Proof

Prophet Yusuf ﷺ preferred prison incarceration over committing indecency:

﴿ قَالَ رَبِّ السِّجْنُ أَحَبُّ إِلَيَّ مِمَّا يَدْعُونَنِي إِلَيْهِ ۖ وَإِلَّا تَصْرِفْ عَنِّي كَيْدَهُنَّ
أَصْبُ إِلَيْهِنَّ وَأَكُن مِّنَ الْجَاهِلِينَ ﴾

﴿He said, "My Lord, prison is more to my liking than that to which they invite me. And if You do not avert from me their plan, I might incline toward them and thus be of the ignorant."﴾

[Surah Yusuf 12:33]

This is one of the greatest proofs of Prophet Yusuf's innocence. Why would someone prefer prison over anything he (supposedly) desires? Had he only answered her invitation and obeyed her call to commit indecency, he would not have remained in the prison for several years (*biḍ'u*)[14] because of the subsequent accusations with which she levelled against him.

Thus, the allegation that Yusuf had an evil interest in the wife of the minister is patently false. This is understood by every fair-minded individual who studies the history of this Noble Prophet and understands the meanings of the Quran.

The Fifth Proof

The praise of Allah Most High for Prophet Yusuf ﷺ in several places throughout various surahs in the Quran, as Allah said:

﴿ كَذَٰلِكَ لِنَصْرِفَ عَنْهُ السُّوءَ وَالْفَحْشَاءَ إِنَّهُ مِنْ عِبَادِنَا الْمُخْلَصِينَ ﴾

﴿And she certainly determined to seduce him, and he would have inclined to her had he not seen the proof of his Lord. And thus it was that We should avert from him evil and immorality. Indeed, he was of Our chosen servants.﴾

[Surah Yusuf 12:24]

Allah said in the middle of this story:

﴿ وَلَمَّا بَلَغَ أَشُدَّهُ آتَيْنَاهُ حُكْمًا وَعِلْمًا وَكَذَٰلِكَ نَجْزِي الْمُحْسِنِينَ
وَرَاوَدَتْهُ الَّتِي هُوَ فِي بَيْتِهَا عَن نَّفْسِهِ ﴾

﴿And when Joseph reached maturity, We gave him judgment and knowledge. And thus We reward the doers of good. And she, in whose house he was, sought to seduce him.﴾

[Surah Yusuf 12:22-23]

---

[14] The Arabic word *biḍ'u* means a duration from anywhere between 3 to 9 years. [t]

Allah Most High has declared about him that he is amongst the doers-of-excellence and that he is amongst His sincere servants whom Allah chose for Prophethood and had selected them to obey Him and His worship. Will the praise of Allah ﷻ be upon anyone except he who purifies his soul, and cleanses his thoughts from every evil intention and every loathsome action, thereby becoming among the purest of those brought-nigh? The Messenger of Allah ﷺ also bore witness for his righteousness and Godfearingness, as well as his purity and uprightness when he ﷺ said:

(إِنَّ الْكَرِيمَ ابْنَ الْكَرِيمِ ابْنِ الْكَرِيمِ يُوسُفُ بْنُ يَعْقُوبَ بْنِ إِسْحَاقَ بْنِ إِبْرَاهِيمَ)

"Indeed, the noble one (al-karīm), the son of the noble one, the son of the noble one; Yusūf the son of Yaqub, the son of Isḥāq, the son of Ibrahim.

This endorsement is sufficient to prove his nobility and virtue.

The Sixth Proof

In a gathering of women from the city, the minister's wife confessed to the innocence of Prophet Yusuf ﵇ and his chastity, as Allah Most High said:

﴿ فَلَمَّا رَأَيْنَهُ أَكْبَرْنَهُ وَقَطَّعْنَ أَيْدِيَهُنَّ وَقُلْنَ حَاشَ لِلَّهِ مَا هَٰذَا بَشَرًا إِنْ هَٰذَا إِلَّا مَلَكٌ كَرِيمٌ ۝ قَالَتْ فَذَٰلِكُنَّ الَّذِي لُمْتُنَّنِي فِيهِ ۖ وَلَقَدْ رَاوَدتُّهُ عَن نَّفْسِهِ فَاسْتَعْصَمَ ۖ ﴾

﴿And when they saw him, they greatly admired him and cut their hands and said, "How perfect is Allah! This is not a man; this is none but a noble angel." She said, "That is the one about whom you blamed me. And I certainly sought to seduce him, but he firmly refused;"﴾

[Surah Yusuf 12:31-32]

This is an explicit testimony for the chastity of Yusuf ﵇ and his exoneration from the very wife of the minister who accused him in front of her husband of committing indecency. The semantic field of the Arabic verb (in the tenth verb pattern) *ista ʿṣama* connotes meanings of 'powerful restraint' and 'intense perseverance' as if he was divinely protected from the affair while he was simultaneously striving to avoid it. That is an obvious elucidation that Yusuf ﵇ *is* innocent from what some people interpreted *interest* and *proof* to mean, and we have explained its patent falsehood earlier.

The Seventh Proof

Numerous signs appeared to prove the innocence of Yusuf ﷺ which contained obvious evidences in front of all to see. Despite that, the minister of Egypt still sentenced him to prison to make it seem to the people that Yusuf was guilty and to cover-up his wife, as Allah Most High said:

﴿ثُمَّ بَدَا لَهُم مِّن بَعْدِ مَا رَأَوُا الْآيَاتِ لَيَسْجُنُنَّهُ حَتَّىٰ حِينٍ﴾

❨Then it appeared to them after they had seen the signs that the minister should surely imprison him for a time.❩

[Surah Yusuf 12:35]

ʿAllāmah al-Nasafī ؒ said in his *tafsir*:

> The following Words of Allah ❨...then it became clear to them...❩ means it became apparent to them. The pronoun *them* refers to the minister and his family. Thereafter, Allah said ❨...after they saw the signs...❩ which are the proofs for the innocence of Yusuf like the ripping of his shirt, the women cutting their hands, the testimony of an infant and others. Then Allah said ❨...he should definitely imprison him...❩ to present an excuse and to stop people from gossiping. This was nothing other than a wife putting her husband in his place. He was obedient to her; she had him wrapped around her pinky finger. Allah's Word ❨...until a time-appointed...❩ refers to her wanting to imprison Prophet Yusuf ﷺ for a while to see what he will do.

The Eighth Proof

Allah ﷻ answered Yusuf's supplication when he prayed to his Lord to avert the machination and evil plotting of the women against him. And if he desired to obey the minister's wife, he would not have begged Allah to avert their plots from him, as Allah said:

﴿فَاسْتَجَابَ لَهُ رَبُّهُ فَصَرَفَ عَنْهُ كَيْدَهُنَّ ۚ إِنَّهُ هُوَ السَّمِيعُ الْعَلِيمُ﴾

❨So his Lord responded to him and averted from him their plan. Indeed, He is the Hearing, the Knowing.❩

[Surah Yusuf 12:34]

The Ninth Proof

Another proof of the infallibility of Prophet Yusuf ﷺ is his refusal to be released from the prison until his innocence was publicly proclaimed in front of all people. That indicates his high-degree of sagacity, chastity, and his impeccable character. Were that not that case, he would not have preferred to remain in the prison after he had lingered there for seven to nine years and encountered hardships. He did not accept to be released from the prison until everyone was convinced of his innocence:

﴿ وَقَالَ الْمَلِكُ ائْتُونِي بِهِ فَلَمَّا جَاءَهُ الرَّسُولُ قَالَ ارْجِعْ إِلَى رَبِّكَ ﴾

﴿And the king said, "Bring him to me." But when the messenger came to him, [Joseph] said, "Return to your master...﴾

[Surah Yusuf 12:50]

i.e. your master, the minister of Egypt.

﴿فَاسْأَلْهُ مَا بَالُ النِّسْوَةِ اللَّاتِي قَطَّعْنَ أَيْدِيَهُنَّ إِنَّ رَبِّي بِكَيْدِهِنَّ عَلِيمٌ﴾

﴿...and ask him what is the case of the women who cut their hands. Indeed, my Lord is Knowing of their plan.﴾

[Surah Yusuf 12:50]

The Tenth Proof

And lastly, the tenth proof is the clear and explicit confession from both the group of women, as well as the wife of the minister who accused him. It does not leave an iota of doubt in the innocence of Yusuf, his blemishlessness, and his infallibility from what was attributed to him. That incident occurred when the minister's wife gathered the women of the city and asked them about the veracious Yusuf and they responded to him with an explicit, definitive answer:

﴿ قَالَ مَا خَطْبُكُنَّ إِذْ رَاوَدتُّنَّ يُوسُفَ عَن نَّفْسِهِ ۚ قُلْنَ حَاشَ لِلَّهِ مَا عَلِمْنَا عَلَيْهِ
مِن سُوءٍ ۚ قَالَتِ امْرَأَتُ الْعَزِيزِ الْآنَ حَصْحَصَ الْحَقُّ أَنَا رَاوَدتُّهُ عَن نَّفْسِهِ وَإِنَّهُ لَمِنَ
الصَّادِقِينَ ذَٰلِكَ لِيَعْلَمَ أَنِّي لَمْ أَخُنْهُ بِالْغَيْبِ وَأَنَّ اللَّهَ لَا يَهْدِي كَيْدَ الْخَائِنِينَ ﴾

﴿Said [the king to the women], "What was your condition when you sought to seduce Joseph?" They said, "How perfect is Allah! We know about him no evil." The wife of the minister said, "Now the truth has become evident."﴾

i.e. it is exposed and manifest.

﴿ أَنَا رَاوَدتُّهُ عَن نَّفْسِهِ وَإِنَّهُ لَمِنَ الصَّادِقِينَ ذَٰلِكَ لِيَعْلَمَ أَنِّي لَمْ أَخُنْهُ بِالْغَيْبِ وَأَنَّ
اللَّهَ لَا يَهْدِي كَيْدَ الْخَائِنِينَ ﴾

﴿It was I who sought to seduce him, and indeed, he is of the truthful. That is

so the minister will know that I did not betray him in [his] absence and that Allah does not guide the plan of the treacherous.﴿

[Surah Yusuf 12:51-52]

These are but ten reasons for the infallibility of the veracious Yusuf ﷺ and his innocence from the false-testimony and slander that was ascribed to him that I derived from the Quran. And Allah speaks the truth, and He guides to the right path.

Chapter Seven

What has been Narrated about Prophet Nuh ﷺ

Of the verses about the story of Prophet Nuh ﷺ is Allah Most High's word:

﴿وَنَادَى نُوحٌ رَبَّهُ فَقَالَ رَبِّ إِنَّ ابْنِي مِنْ أَهْلِي وَإِنَّ وَعْدَكَ الْحَقُّ وَأَنْتَ أَحْكَمُ الْحَاكِمِينَ ﴾ ﴿ قَالَ يَا نُوحُ إِنَّهُ لَيْسَ مِنْ أَهْلِكَ إِنَّهُ عَمَلٌ غَيْرُ صَالِحٍ فَلَا تَسْأَلْنِ مَا لَيْسَ لَكَ بِهِ عِلْمٌ إِنِّي أَعِظُكَ أَنْ تَكُونَ مِنَ الْجَاهِلِينَ﴾

﴿And Noah called to his Lord and said, "My Lord, indeed my son is of my family; and indeed, Your promise is true; and You are the most just of judges!﴾ ﴿He said, "O Noah, indeed he is not of your family; indeed, he is [one whose] work was other than righteous, so ask Me not for that about which you have no knowledge. Indeed, I advise you, lest you be among the ignorant.﴾

[Surah Hud 11:45-46]

Nuh ﷺ only asked his Lord to save his son because Allah ﷻ promised him He would save his family and destroy the wrong-doers. His son was from his family and had promised Nuh that he would have faith. So Nuh ﷺ begged Allah to save his son from the deluge believing that his son was following his religion. But he did not recognise the reality of his son's disbelief except after Allah Most High manifested it with His words: ﴿*...indeed he is not of your family;*﴾ [Surah Nuh 11:46] i.e. he is not from your family whom I promised to save because he is not a believer. I promised to save the believers. At that, Nuh absolved himself from his son.

Furthermore, Nuh ﷺ did not commit any disobedience here or sin, he only prayed to Allah to save his son. Fatherly compassion and love gripped him, and he sought from Allah to inspire his son with faith so he could be saved from the deluge. So Allah Most High informed him that his damnation is foreknown, and he will be of those destroyed.

Shaykh Abū Mansur ﷺ states about the exegesis (*tafsir*) of this verse:

According to Nuh ﷺ, his son was following his religion [Islam], but in reality, he was a hypocrite. Otherwise, Nuh would not have said '*my son is from my family'* and ask Allah for his salvation while Allah had already prohibited beseeching for things like this when Allah ﷻ said:

﴿ وَلَا تُخَاطِبْنِي فِي الَّذِينَ ظَلَمُوا إِنَّهُم مُّغْرَقُونَ ﴾

﴿...and do not address Me concerning those who have wronged; indeed, they are to be drowned.﴾

[Surah Hud 11:37]

So Nuh ﷺ only asked about was apparent to him [regarding his son] just as the hypocrites used to give a similar false impression to our Prophet ﷺ, while they internally harboured ill-feelings towards him. And he ﷺ did not know about that until Allah Most High brought it forth to him with His words:

﴿ لَيْسَ مِنْ أَهْلِكَ ﴾

﴿...indeed he is not of your family;﴾

[Surah Nuh 11:46]

i.e. not from those whom I have promised to save. The true believers are those who believe both in secret and in private.

Chapter Eight

What was Transmitted about Prophet Yunus ﷺ

Of the verses about the story of Prophet Yunus is Allah Most High's word:

﴿ وَذَا النُّونِ إِذ ذَّهَبَ مُغَاضِبًا فَظَنَّ أَن لَّن نَّقْدِرَ عَلَيْهِ فَنَادَىٰ فِي الظُّلُمَاتِ أَن لَّا إِلَٰهَ إِلَّا أَنتَ سُبْحَانَكَ إِنِّي كُنتُ مِنَ الظَّالِمِينَ
فَاسْتَجَبْنَا لَهُ وَنَجَّيْنَاهُ مِنَ الْغَمِّ ۚ وَكَذَٰلِكَ نُنجِي الْمُؤْمِنِينَ ﴾

﴿*And [mention] the man of the fish, when he went off in anger and thought that We would not decree [anything] upon him. And he called out within the darknesses, "There is no deity except You; exalted are You. Indeed, I have been of the wrongdoers. So We responded to him and saved him from the distress. And thus do We save the believers."*﴾

[Surah Anbiyā' 21:87-88]

The Incorrect Interpretation

These verses might outwardly give the impression that Yunus ﷺ had done what angered Allah ﷻ and that he doubted the Power of Allah to avenge his action. This is an incorrect understanding and an explanation of these verses that is incorrect. Some of the nescient have fallen into this misunderstanding and thought that Yunus ﷺ had fallen into disobedience, disobeyed the command of Allah and departed while angry with his Lord. So the whale swallowed him because of this 'sin.'

The Correct Interpretation

The correct understanding is what the scholars of exegesis have mentioned about the meaning of these verses, that Yunus ﷺ had warned his community of the punishment of Allah if they did not believe. But they persisted in their misguidance and disbelief, so he promised them an impending punishment. When the punishment was delayed, he departed from them like someone hiding from them, disappearing from their sight because of the respite being given to them.

He feared that they would mock and denigrate him, and accuse him of lying against Allah because he informed them of an imminent punishment to descend, yet it did not descend. So he left angered with his community, not angered with his Lord. God forbid, he would never do that! He would never be angry with his Lord or disobey his command.

Shaykh Abu'l-Barakāt ʿAbdullāh al-Nasafi ؓ said in his *tafsir* about Allah's words:

> The word *'Dhu-nūn'* means 'whale' and this verse means, 'mention the companion of the whale' [i.e. the one associated with the whale]:
>
> ﴿ وَذَا النُّونِ إِذ ذَّهَبَ مُغَاضِبًا ﴾
>
> ﴿*And mention the man of the fish [Dhu-nūn], when he went off in anger.*﴾
>
> [Surah 'Anbiyā' 21:87]

He continues to say: the words of Allah ﴿*when he went off in anger*﴾ means that he went off begrudging his community. His anger with his community means he angered them by his absence from them, because of their fear of the punishment becoming unleashed if he left. It is narrated that he felt constrained by their belying him after such a long time of warning them, but they did not pay heed and grew firm in their disbelief. Thus, he begrudged them and thought he was justified in doing so. He did not do so except by having righteous indignation for Allah's sake and for loathing disbelief and its people. However, he ought to have exercised firm patience until the permission from Allah Most High was issued to migrate from them, and he was tested by being in the belly of the whale.

Thus, his anger was directed towards his community, not his Lord. And his censuring was due to the absence of patience and his leaving his people without permission from Allah Most High. So in this vein, Allah commanded His Prophet Muhammad ﷺ to bear patience in the face of the rejection of the polytheists, to not have a constricted heart and to exercise great patience like the situation of Yunus ؑ with his people to the extent that Allah struck a parable of Yunus ؑ in the Holy Quran. Allah said:

﴿ فَاصْبِرْ لِحُكْمِ رَبِّكَ وَلَا تَكُن كَصَاحِبِ الْحُوتِ إِذْ نَادَىٰ وَهُوَ مَكْظُومٌ
لَّوْلَا أَن تَدَارَكَهُ نِعْمَةٌ مِّن رَّبِّهِ لَنُبِذَ بِالْعَرَاءِ وَهُوَ مَذْمُومٌ فَاجْتَبَاهُ رَبُّهُ فَجَعَلَهُ مِنَ
الصَّالِحِينَ ﴾

﴾*Then be patient for the decision of your Lord, [O Muhammad], and be not like the companion of the fish when he cried out while he was distressed. Were it not that a favour from his Lord overtook him, he would have been thrown onto the naked shore while he was censured. And his Lord chose him and made him of the righteous.*﴿

[Surah Qalam 68:48-49]

Allah Most High's Word: ﴾*...he would have been thrown onto the naked shore while he was censured*﴿ is the answer to ﴾*...were it not...*﴿. It is common knowledge that ﴾*...were it not...*﴿ in the Arabic language is a conditional sentence when something is actually present. In other words, the presence of the condition prevents the answer from occurring. Thus, rendering the meaning of the noble verse as follows:

If Allah had not blessed him by answering his supplication and accepting his excuse he would have remained in the belly of the whale (*bi al-ʿarā'*) i.e. in the wilderness, while he was blameworthy. He was rebuked for his mistake. However, Allah showed him mercy so he was cast out without blame.

As for Allah Most High's Word: ﴾*...and thought that We would not decree anything [qadara] upon him*﴿, it refers to his believing that leaving his people would not warrant rebuke, and not that Allah was not able to punish him, as Ibn ʿAbbās ؓ reported.

Ibn ʿAbbās ؓ narrated that one day he entered upon Muʿāwiyah ؓ and Muʿāwiyah said to him:

> 'Once the waves of the ocean were smashing my ship and I was going to be shipwrecked by it. I could not find any way out of the situation except through you.' So Ibn ʿAbbās ؓ asked: 'So what happened, O Muʿāwiyah?' So he read the verse ﴾*...and thought that We would not decree anything (qadara) upon him*﴿ and said: 'Did the Prophet of Allah (Yunus) think that his Lord was not capable of chastising him?' Ibn ʿAbbās ؓ corrected his understanding of that verse in the Quran stating: 'The use of the word *qadara* refers to rebuking (*qadar*), not capability (*qudra*).' Thus, this Quranic verse actually carries the following meaning: 'He (Yunus) thought that We would not rebuke (lit. constrict) him (*qadara*) for leaving his people without Our permission.' Allah Most High uses the same word in another verse saying:

﴿ وَأَمَّا إِذَا مَا ابْتَلَاهُ فَقَدَرَ عَلَيْهِ رِزْقَهُ فَيَقُولُ رَبِّي أَهَانَنِ ﴾

﴾*But when He tries him and <u>constricts</u> his provision, he says, "My Lord has humiliated me."*﴿

[Surah Fajr 89:16]

Chapter Nine

Was the Messenger of Allah ﷺ made to make Mistakes?

The Messenger of Allah ﷺ - like all the Noble Prophets – is divinely protected from sins and iniquities, guarded by the divine concern of Allah ﷻ, and surrounded by His custodianship. It is not possible for violations of the sacred commands of Allah to emanate from them, or to commit sins which deserve censure.

However, at times he ﷺ did exert his judgment and act contrary to the most virtuous and most excellent course; subsequently his Lord rebuked him. This is not connected to sins and disobedience; it is only a way of drawing attention to an act that would be more perfect and more virtuous which is expressed in the saying of some of the scholars:

حَسَنَاتُ الْأَبْرَارِ سَيِّئَاتُ الْمُقَرَّبِينَ

The good deeds of the pious are the evil deeds for those brought-nigh.

Ten Verses about the 'Censure' of the Messenger of Allah ﷺ and their Correct Interpretation

We will present some of the transmitted texts which contain ostensible 'rebuke' for the Messenger of Allah ﷺ, and we will explain the correct view about, just as we will present other texts which ostensibly suggest that the Messenger ﷺ fell into contravention and disobedience. We will elucidate its meanings in the light of the statements of the Imams of *tafsir*, and in the light of the Book and the Sunna. So we declare—and from Allah we seek aid.

THE FIRST VERSE

Ostensible censure regarding the Captives of Badr

As for the first verse that ostensibly contains censure of the Messenger ﷺ that could be misinterpreted as the Noble Prophet contravening the command of Allah and performing what did not please Allah:

﴿ مَا كَانَ لِنَبِيٍّ أَن يَكُونَ لَهُ أَسْرَى حَتَّى يُثْخِنَ فِي الأَرْضِ تُرِيدُونَ عَرَضَ الدُّنْيَا وَاللّهُ يُرِيدُ الآخِرَةَ وَاللّهُ عَزِيزٌ حَكِيمٌ (٦٧) لَّوْلاَ كِتَابٌ مِّنَ اللّهِ سَبَقَ لَمَسَّكُمْ فِيمَا أَخَذْتُمْ عَذَابٌ عَظِيمٌ ﴾

﴿It is not for a prophet to have captives [of war] until he inflicts a massacre [upon Allah 's enemies] in the land. Some of you desire the commodities of this world, but Allah desires [for you] the Hereafter. And Allah is Exalted in Might and Wise. If not for a decree from Allah that preceded, you would have been touched for what you took by a great punishment.﴾

[Surah Anfāl 8:87-68]

Perhaps some of the nescient believe that the Messenger ﷺ committed sins or perpetrated crimes, or disobeyed an order from the Lord of the worlds which merited the revelation of this apparently severe rebuke. Even though, in reality, the matter is not as they surmise. The most that can be drawn from this was that the Messenger ﷺ had sought counsel from some of his Companions about the captives of Badr. Then he exerted his judgment about their matter and selected the opinion of the majority. Thus, he accepted the ransom [for freedom] from the captives. This was him ﷺ exercising judgment which was against the most virtuous, most excellent and preferred way because the overall benefit of the summons to Allah and the overall benefit of Islam dictated that he ﷺ should not accept the ransom.

Rather, he should have shed their blood to weaken the thorn of disbelief and to break the resolve of the polytheists[15] so that honour and victory would only be for the servants of Allah, the believers. Especially, since this was the first battle that occurred between the believers and the polytheists.

---

[15] The polytheists here refer to those who broke their treaty with the Muslim State and were blatantly treacherous.

We will mention some narrations here from the scholars of a type of exegesis called 'exegesis by transmission' (*tafsir bi al-ma'thūr*) about why these verses were revealed:

Tirmidhī, Ḥākim and Bayhaqī narrate that Ibn Mas'ūd ﷺ said,

"On the day of Badr, captives were brought.[16]

Abu Bakr ﷺ said, 'O Messenger of Allah, they are your people, your family. Release them, perhaps Allah will forgive them.'

'Umar ﷺ said, 'O Messenger of Allah, they belied you, they exiled you, and they fought against you—put them forward and execute them.'

'Abdullah ibn Rawāḥah ﷺ said, 'Look for a valley with plenty of dried wood and burn them in a fire.'

So 'Abbās ﷺ said while hearing what they were saying, '[Were you to do so,] you will sever your family ties.'

So the Prophet ﷺ retreated to his tent and he did not respond to them whatsoever. So some people said: 'He agrees with the opinion of Abu Bakr ﷺ.' Still some said 'He agrees with the opinion of 'Umar ﷺ.' So the Messenger Allah ﷺ exited and said,

(إن الله ليلين قلوب رجال حتى تكون ألين من اللبن. وإن الله ليشدد قلوب رجال حتى تكون أشد من الحجارة)

Truly, Allah will soften the hearts of men until they become softer than yogurt. Indeed, Allah will harden the hearts of men until they become harder than stone.

Your example, O Abu Bakr, is like that of Ibrahim ﷺ when He said,

﴿ فَمَن تَبِعَنِي فَإِنَّهُ مِنِّي ۖ وَمَنْ عَصَانِي فَإِنَّكَ غَفُورٌ رَّحِيمٌ ﴾

﴾*...so whoever follows me - then he is of me; and whoever disobeys me - indeed, You are [yet] Forgiving and Merciful.*﴿

[Surah Ibrahim 14:36]

And your example, O Abu Bakr, is like that of 'Īsā ﷺ when he said,

﴿ إِن تُعَذِّبْهُمْ فَإِنَّهُمْ عِبَادُكَ ۖ وَإِن تَغْفِرْ لَهُمْ فَإِنَّكَ أَنتَ الْعَزِيزُ الْحَكِيمُ ﴾

﴾*If You should punish them - indeed they are Your servants; but if You forgive them - indeed it is You who is the Exalted in Might, the Wise.*﴿

[Surah Mā'ida 5:118]

---

[16] That is, hostile enemies of the state.

And your example, O ʿUmar, is like that of Nuh ﷺ when he said,

﴿ رَّبِّ لَا تَذَرْ عَلَى الْأَرْضِ مِنَ الْكَافِرِينَ دَيَّارًا ﴾

﴾My Lord, do not leave upon the earth from among the disbelievers an inhabitant.﴿

[Surah Nuh 71:26]

And your example, O ʿUmar, is like that of Mūsā ﷺ when he said,

﴿رَبَّنَا اطْمِسْ عَلَىٰ أَمْوَالِهِمْ وَاشْدُدْ عَلَىٰ قُلُوبِهِمْ فَلَا يُؤْمِنُوا حَتَّىٰ يَرَوُا الْعَذَابَ الْأَلِيمَ﴾

﴾Our Lord, obliterate their wealth and harden their hearts so that they will not believe until they see the painful punishment﴿

[Surah Yunus 10:88]

Then he ﷺ said, "All of you are related to us, so none of you will be released except by ransom or execution."

So ʿAbdullah said: "O Messenger of Allah, except Suhayl ibn Bayḍā' because I heard him mentioning Islam.[17] So Messenger of Allah ﷺ became silent. And you have never seen me on any day anyone more frightened that stones were going to be pelted at me than that day until Messenger of Allah ﷺ said, "Except Suhayl ibn Bayḍā. Then Allah Most High revealed the verse:

﴿ مَا كَانَ لِنَبِيٍّ أَنْ يَكُونَ لَهُ أَسْرَىٰ حَتَّىٰ يُثْخِنَ فِي الْأَرْضِ... ﴾

﴾It is not for a prophet to have captives [of war] until he inflicts a massacre [upon Allah 's enemies] in the land...﴿"

[Surah Anfāl 8:67]

The Second Narration

It is narrated by Aḥmad and Muslim from the *hadith* of Ibn ʿAbbās ﷺ:

When the captives were captured, referring to the Day of Badr, Messenger of Allah ﷺ said to Abu Bakr ﷺ and ʿUmar ﷺ, 'What do you think we should do with these captives?' Abu Bakr ﷺ said, 'O Messenger of Allah, they are our cousins and our close relatives, we think you should take a ransom [in exchange] for them so it will be leverage for us against the disbelievers. Perhaps Allah will guide them to Islam.' The Messenger of Allah ﷺ said, 'What do you think, O Son of Khaṭṭāb?'

[17] That is, he was talking about embracing Islam.

He replied, 'No, I swear by Allah, O Messenger of Allah, I don't see it the same way Abu Bakr does. Rather, I think we should seize the opportunity, take control and execute them. So ʿAlī should take ʿAqīl (his brother) and execute him, and I should take so-and-so and execute him ('Umar's relative), and so-and-so should take so-and-so his relative because these ones are the leaders of disbelief and their advocates.'

So the Messenger of Allah ﷺ inclined towards what Abu Bakr ؓ said and he did not incline to what I said. So when the morrow came, I approached and noticed the Messenger of Allah ﷺ and Abu Bakr sitting and weeping. I said, 'O Messenger of Allah, inform me what is making you cry and your companion,[18] so if I can cry, I will. And if I cannot cry, I will make myself cry because both of you are crying! The Messenger of Allah ﷺ said: "Cry over what your companion [i.e. meaning himself] opined about accepting ransom for them. It has been shown to me that their punishment should be closer than this tree (a tree that was very close to him). Then Allah revealed the verse:

﴿ مَا كَانَ لِنَبِيٍّ أَنْ يَكُونَ لَهُ أَسْرَى حَتَّى يُثْخِنَ فِي الْأَرْضِ... ﴾

﴾*It is not for a prophet to have captives [of war] until he inflicts a massacre [upon Allah 's enemies] in the land...*﴿"

[Surah Anfāl 8:87]

This hadith indicates that those who opined to the Messenger of Allah ﷺ to accept the ransom were the majority. Most of the narrations only mention Abu Bakr ؓ because he was the first to opine that, and the Messenger of Allah used to seek his opinion first when seeking counsel from his Companions as is known that he is the greatest of them in rank and the most beloved to the Messenger of Allah ﷺ.

The purpose of this stern censure from Allah ﷻ to His Prophet ﷺ and his righteous Companions was to teach and warn them to take the more perfect and more virtuous way, and to take their time in determining intricate matters like these. So Allah ﷻ desired honour for Islam and to exalt its standing.

ʿAbdullah b. ʿAbbās ؓ explained that the words of Allah Most High ﴾*It is not for a prophet to have captives [of war] until he inflicts a massacre [upon Allah 's enemies] in the land...*﴿ specifically refer to the Battle of Badr, because at that time the Muslims were few in number.

[18] Here *Your companion* refers to Abu Bakr ؓ.

When they grew in number and gained authority, Allah revealed about the captives:

﴿ فَإِمَّا مَنًّا بَعْدُ وَإِمَّا فِدَاءً ﴾

﴾...either confer favour afterwards or ransom [them].﴿

[Surah Muhammad 47:4].

So Allah gave the Prophet ﷺ and the believers a choice about the captives: if you wish, you may kill them, if you wish, take them as slaves, or if you wish, ransom them (i.e. set them free by accepting a ransom). While the verse indicates that this matter was decided by the Messenger deliberating, exercising judgment, and consulting his Companions, nevertheless, Allah's Pre-Eternal Wisdom decreed that the believers should not be responsible for their error in judgment. Thus, Allah concludes by declaring:

﴿ لَوْلَا كِتَابٌ مِنَ اللهِ سَبَقَ لَمَسَّكُمْ فِيمَا أَخَذْتُمْ عَذَابٌ عَظِيمٌ ﴾

﴾If not for a decree from Allah that preceded, you would have been touched for what you decided by a great punishment.﴿

[Surah Anfāl 8:68]

THE SECOND VERSE

Ostensible censure for giving permission to the hypocrites

﴿ عَفَا اللَّهُ عَنكَ لِمَ أَذِنتَ لَهُمْ حَتَّىٰ يَتَبَيَّنَ لَكَ الَّذِينَ صَدَقُوا وَتَعْلَمَ الْكَاذِبِينَ ﴾

❴*May Allah pardon you, [O Messenger of Allah]; why did you give them permission [to remain behind] before it was evident to you who were the truthful and who were the liars?*❵

[Surah Tawba 9:34]

This verse does not contain anything which indicates to the Messenger of Allah ﷺ falling into sin. The upshot of this verse was Allah ﷻ rebuked him for giving permission to some of the hypocrites to abandon joining a military campaign when they presented their excuses of being incapable to join. As a result, a censure was revealed by Allah ﷻ to him ﷺ.

Sufyan ibn ʿUyayna ؒ said, "Look to this gentleness! Allah began by pardoning the Prophet ﷺ before He rebuked him for a mistake."

ʿAmr ibn Maymūn ؒ said, "There are two things the Prophet ﷺ did that he was not commanded to do; granting permission to the hypocrites and taking ransom from the captives of Badr. So, Allah censured him ﷺ as you all hear [in the Quran]."

Some of the scholars of *tafsir* narrate that the verse does not even indicate to rebuke, much less falling into sin, because Allah ﷻ revered him and raised his rank by beginning the discourse with praying for blessings for him ﷺ just like how a man speaks to someone noble who he is addressing by saying: 'May Allah pardon you, you didn't take care of my need?' and 'May Allah be pleased with you, won't you visit me?'

This is what Imams Rāzī and Baghawī ؒ and others opined. On the other hand, Imam Zamakhshari ؒ showed poor manners in his *tafsir* about the Words of Allah Most High to His Prophet ﷺ:

﴿ عَفَا اللَّهُ عَنكَ ﴾

❴*May Allah pardon you, [O Muhammad]; why did you give them permission [to remain behind]...?*❵

[Surah Tawba 9:34]

Such that he said the following:

> The Words of Allah ❴*May Allah pardon you...*❵ indicate to a crime because pardoning [typically] follows a crime. Thus, the verse means:

> you made a mistake and what a wretched thing you have done.
>
> The following portion of the verse ﴾*...why did you give them permission?*﴿ elucidates what was indicated before by *'pardoning'* and it means: 'What is the matter with you? Why did you grant them permission to remain behind from the military campaign when they sought your permission and presented you with excuses?'
>
> 'Why did you not delay ﴾*...until it became evident to you*﴿ who was honest when presenting their excuses from those who were lying?'

The author of *Tafsir al-Manār* mentioned a subtle point that is exceptionally precise when he said:

> Indeed, some of the scholars of *tafsir*—especially Zamakhsharī—have shown bad manners in the way they interpreted Allah Most High's pardoning the Messenger of Allah ﷺ in this verse.
>
> It was imperative for them to learn the highest manners with the Prophet ﷺ from this incident. Especially since his Lord and Educator [Allah] informed him of his pardon *before* the mistake which displays the utmost ennoblement and gentleness. Some others like Imam Rāzī, exaggerated to the other extreme when they wanted to establish that *pardoning* does not indicate a mistake at all. And the most we can say is the *giving of permission* which Allah rebuked him for was out of being contrary to the best course of action.

Then he said:

> The Arabic word for 'sin' (*dhanb*) is not synonymous with disobedience. It is nothing other than any action that results in harm or foregoes the overall good. It is linguistically derived from the tail of an animal. And the *granting of permission* that was forgiven occurred because of the Prophet ﷺ foregoing the overall good which was related in the verse, namely clarifying who was truthful and who was lying.

The *giving of permission* that he was censured for was due to exercising his judgment where no explicit text was revealed. It is permissible and occurs from the Prophets عليهم السلام because they are not divinely protected from mistakes. The Divine protection that is indisputable only applies to conveying the revelation, elucidating it, and acting according to it. Hence, it is impossible for the Messengers عليهم السلام to lie or commit mistakes about what they convey about their Lord, or contradict it in deed. The scholars of foundational principles have explicitly stated that mistakes are possible when Prophets exercise their judgment. They said, however, Allah will not allow them to persist in therein. Rather,

He clarifies to them the correct way regarding it. Thus, the upshot of this entire issue is that there *was* a contravention that necessitated rigidity in rebuke. But because of the gentleness of the Lord, the Subtle, All-Aware of His Messenger, who is the giver of glad-tidings and the warner, He informed him of pardoning him before explaining to him.

THE THIRD VERSE

The Prophet's ﷺ frowning and turning away

$$\text{عَبَسَ وَتَوَلَّى أَنْ جَاءَهُ الْأَعْمَى}$$

❮*He frowned and turned away.*❯

[Surah ʿAbasa 80:1]

Those who believe that the Prophets ﷺ commit acts of disobedience and that infallibility is not obligatory for them, have rabidly clung to the outward meaning of these verses [related to this incident], and this is a misinterpretation and a misunderstanding of the verse's correct meaning. Among the reasons for the revelation of this verse is clarifying that the Messenger of Allah ﷺ did not commit an act of disobedience, but rather only acted contrary to what was superior. Thus, Allah Most High alerted him to the more complete and virtuous way. Ibn Jarīr narrated that Ibn ʿAbbās ؓ said that:

> The Messenger of Allah ﷺ was having a private discussion with ʿUtbah b. Rabīʿah, Abū Jahl b. Hishām and al-ʿAbbās b. ʿAbd al-Muṭṭalib ؓ. He used to devote a great deal of time to them and was eager for them to believe. Once, while the Prophet ﷺ was privately discussing with them, a blind man came walking to him ﷺ named ʿAbdullah b. Maktūm ؓ. ʿAbdullah b. Maktūm started asking the Prophet ﷺ to recite a particular verse from the Quran and said: "O Messenger of Allah, teach me of what Allah taught you." So the Messenger of Allah ﷺ turned away from him, frowned his face, and turned towards the Quraysh. So Allah revealed ❮*He frowned and turned away*❯ [Surah ʿAbasa 80:1-2]. Now, when what was revealed about ʿAbdullah b. Maktūm was revealed, the Messenger of Allah ﷺ thenceforth honoured him and would say to him, 'What can I do for you? Do you need anything?" And when those who were with the Prophet went away he ﷺ would still say to him: 'Do you need anything?'

Ibn Jarīr ؓ said: "The fact of mentioning his blindness [in the verse] increases the disapproval as if to say: 'He ﷺ turned away *because* he was blind while that should have increased him in kindness and gentleness, and bringing him close and welcoming him.'"

Now you can understand clearly from the reason of the revelation that the Messenger ﷺ was pre-occupied with the leaders of Quraysh. He ﷺ was avid at inviting them to Islam because if they were to embrace Islam, then due to their Islam, their entire community would embrace Islam. This blind companion ؓ came at a time that the Messenger ﷺ was busy inviting them to Islam and he did not answer for any other reason other than what was—in his estimation—of more importance and greater significance. So Allah censured him for that and explained to him ﷺ what was better and more excellent.

Imam Rāzī said:

> Those who say that sins emanate from the Prophet ﷺ have latched on to this verse and said Allah's rebuking him ﷺ for that action indicates that this action was an act of disobedience. And this is far from the truth because as we have explained, that was obligatory for that specific occasion. There is only one exception that an objector may raise and that is, it could give the 'impression' that the rich were preferred over the poor, and that does not befit the noble persona of the Messenger ﷺ. And were that the case, it would have only occurred out of caution and abandoning the more virtuous and that is not even the smallest sin.

Ibn Ḥazm retorted by saying:

> As for Allah's word ﴾*He frowned and turned away*﴿ [Surah ʿAbasa 80:1], indeed some of the great leaders of the Quraysh had sat with him ﷺ and he hoped for their Islam. He knew that if they embraced Islam, because of their embracing Islam, a multitude of people would accept Islam and Islam would gain ascendancy. He ﷺ also knew that the blind Prophetic Companion who was asking him religious issues would not be absent from him and would always be present with him ﷺ, so he ﷺ was otherwise pre-occupied from him because he feared losing this great good compared to the one who is not feared to be absent from him ﷺ. This shows the utmost foresight in the religion and exercising of good judgment to give victory to the Quran in the most apparent way and to bring about a good outcome, and the result of drawing nearer to Allah which were one of us to do that today, we would be rewarded. So Allah Most High rebuked him ﷺ because it was preferred to Allah to attend to the God-fearing, goodly, and virtuous blind man, and to leave those stubborn people be.

THE FOURTH VERSE

The Unreasonable Request of Bani Thaqif

﴿ وَإِن كَادُواْ لَيَفْتِنُونَكَ عَنِ الَّذِي أَوْحَيْنَا إِلَيْكَ لِتَفْتَرِيَ عَلَيْنَا غَيْرَهُ وَإِذاً لاَّتَّخَذُوكَ خَلِيلاً ﴿٣٧﴾ وَلَوْلاَ أَن ثَبَّتْنَاكَ لَقَدْ كِدتَّ تَرْكَنُ إِلَيْهِمْ شَيْئاً قَلِيلاً ﴾

﴾And indeed, they were about to tempt you away from that which We revealed to you to [make] you invent about Us something else; and then they would have taken you as a friend﴿ ﴾And if We had not strengthened you, you would have almost inclined to them a little.﴿

[Surah Bani Isrā'īl 17:73-75]

This verse apparently indicates that the Messenger ﷺ was becoming intimate with the polytheists and depending upon them. This would have been a great sin especially related to conveying the revelation of Allah, however, this issue has not actually been narrated.

It has been narrated that the actual reason for the revelation of this verse is that the tribe of *Thaqīf* who was residing in Ṭā'if, said to the Prophet ﷺ:

"We will not enter your religion until you give us an exclusive distinction which we can boast with over the Arabs. So do not make *zakat* obligatory for us, nor *jihad*, nor *salah*, and all the usury that we owe to other people should be cancelled, but all the usury other people owe to us, should be paid to us. And if the Arabs question, 'Why did you allow that?' Say: 'Allah commanded me thus....'"

Those people desired that he ﷺ give them what they requested. Then Allah revealed these verses, ﴾*and indeed, they were about to tempt you...*﴿. So you see, the Messenger ﷺ did not answer them, but they simply presented their offer to him ﷺ desiring that he agree to their corrupt desires.

Ibn Kathīr ؒ said the following about this verse:

Allah Most High informed us here of His supporting and strengthening His Messenger ﷺ, of the Prophet's Divine protection and Divine safety from the evil of the wicked and the plots of the corrupt. And that He Most High is the Guardian of his affair and his victory ﷺ, He did not entrust the Prophet ﷺ to anyone among the creation. Rather, Allah is his Guardian, Protector, Supporter, and the One who causes His religion to prevail over whoever will show enmity to him ﷺ and oppose him, whether in the east or west of the earth.

Ostensibly Obeying The Disbelievers And Hypocrites

﴿ يَا أَيُّهَا النَّبِيُّ اتَّقِ اللَّهَ وَلَا تُطِعِ الْكَافِرِينَ وَالْمُنَافِقِينَ إِنَّ اللَّهَ كَانَ عَلِيمًا حَكِيمًا * وَاتَّبِعْ مَا يُوحَى إِلَيْكَ مِنْ رَبِّكَ إِنَّ اللَّهَ كَانَ بِمَا تَعْمَلُونَ خَبِيرًا ﴾

﴿O Prophet, fear Allah and do not obey the disbelievers and the hypocrites. Indeed, Allah is ever Knowing and Wise. And follow that which is revealed to you from your Lord. Indeed Allah is ever, with what you do, Acquainted.﴾

[Surah Aḥzāb 33:1-2]

This verse does not contain anything that indicates that the Messenger ﷺ fell into sin. It is simply an address directed to the leaders of the Muslim Community and those in charge, but is ostensibly addressing him ﷺ. It is intended for his Community just as the president says to the leader of his army: 'Do not be lenient with the enemy! Fight them until they submit to your authority and they surrender to your orders! Do not kill children, women, or the elderly! Do not show fear in front of the enemy nor anxiety....' and so on. So while he is speaking to the leader, he is intending to warn the soldiers. He alerts the commander, but by it, intends the army.

The proof that the target audience of this address is the Muslim Community, and not the personality of the Messenger ﷺ, is that Allah Most High concluded the verse in the plural form: *﴿Indeed Allah is All-Aware of what you all do, <u>(ta'lamūn)</u>﴾* [Surah Aḥzāb 33:2], and he did not say "*of what you do <u>(ta'lamu)</u>.*"

It is akin to Allah Most High's Word:

﴿ يَا أَيُّهَا النَّبِيُّ إِذَا طَلَّقْتُمُ النِّسَاءَ فَطَلِّقُوهُنَّ لِعِدَّتِهِنَّ وَأَحْصُوا الْعِدَّةَ وَاتَّقُوا اللَّهَ رَبَّكُمْ ﴾

﴿O Prophet, when you (plural i.e. Muslims) divorce women, divorce them for [the commencement of] their waiting period and keep count of the waiting period, and fear Allah, your Lord.﴾

[Surah Talāq 65:1]

It is an address to the Community *through* the Messenger ﷺ. Even if we were to assume that the address was to the Messenger ﷺ, that would not indicate whatsoever that the Messenger ﷺ even considered obeying the disbelievers and the hypocrites, or committing an act of disobedience to warrant Allah Most High to command him to fear Allah. The point of this was nothing other than Allah Most High warning him of the plots of the disbelievers and the machinations of the hypocrites, and to disclose to him the sickness of their souls in order for the Messenger ﷺ to be cautious of them and to not be deceived by their sweet words.

It has been narrated that Abu Sufyān, ʿIkrimah b. Abu Jahl, and Abu al-ʿAwar al-Sulamī came to the Prophet ﷺ and said: "Stop mentioning our gods. Instead say: 'They intercede and benefit' and we will leave you and your Lord alone." This became hard on the Prophet ﷺ and upon the believers, to the extent that ʿUmar ؓ—who was present during it all—deliberated slaying them when these verses were revealed.

It is narrated that the people of Mecca petitioned the Prophet ﷺ to cease the invitation to Allah and in return they would give him half of all of their wealth. 'It is narrated also that he was fearful of the hypocrites and the Jews of Medina.' So Allah revealed, ﴾*O Prophet, fear Allah…*﴿

Perceived Doubt of the Prophet

﴿ فَإِنْ كُنْتَ فِي شَكٍّ مِمَّا أَنْزَلْنَا إِلَيْكَ فَاسْأَلِ الَّذِينَ يَقْرَأُونَ الْكِتَابَ مِنْ قَبْلِكَ لَقَدْ جَاءَكَ الْحَقُّ مِنْ رَبِّكَ فَلَا تَكُونَنَّ مِنَ الْمُمْتَرِينَ ﴾

﴿*So if you are in doubt, [O Muhammad], about that which We have revealed to you, then ask those who have been reading the Scripture before you. The truth has certainly come to you from your Lord, so never be among the doubters.*﴾

[Surah Yunus 10:94]

These verses do not contain anything that would suggest the Prophet ﷺ harboured doubt about the revelation which was revealed upon him. Rather, it is a literary device which assumes something farfetched as a basis to preclude it from actually happening as is common in Arab tradition. An example is like what one would say to their child 'If you are really my son, then don't be miserly.' So according to this concept of 'assuming something to preclude it from happening', the meaning of this verse is: 'If, O Muhammad, something of doubt emanated from you—hypothetically—concerning what we have related to you from the stories of the past Prophets like Nuh ﷺ and Ibrahim ﷺ, then ask the learned among the People of the Book who read the book before you because they have certain knowledge about it.'

So the intent here is attributing the rabbis with knowledge, not ascribing the Prophet ﷺ with doubt and misgivings. About this, Ibn ʿAbbās ﷺ said, 'No, I swear by Allah, the Messenger of Allah ﷺ did not doubt for the blink of an eye nor did he ask them anything.' It is narrated that when this verse was revealed, the Noble Messenger ﷺ said, 'I do not doubt, nor will I ask.'

The following related quote is from '*Maḥāsin al-Ta'wīl*':

> This verse should not be interpreted as establishing doubt within the Prophet ﷺ, because a hypothetical situation does not necessitate it actually occurring. For instance, when one says: 'Even if someone had five wives, they should all be dealt with equally....'[19]

---

[19] Having five wives is prohibited in the religion of Islam and is a legally impossible scenario. This is precisely why this hyperbolic situation is used in this case, i.e. to emphasize the literary device which is highlighting—in this case—the importance of treating one's wives equally *even if* one more than the

The secret in this type of statement is establishing multiple proofs and strengthening it to increase the power of certainty and tranquillity of the heart. Likewise, the secret in this type of statement is establishing proofs of what was related in the past, drawing precedents in what was contained in the prior scriptures, and that the Quran confirms what is contained therein. Lastly, this type of statement can be used to describe the priests with firmness in knowledge of the validity of what is currently being revealed to the Messenger of Allah ﷺ in opposition to the polytheists.

It is also said that ostensibly the address is to the Prophet ﷺ, but the intended audience is the listener [or reciter]. Meaning 'If you were, O listener, in doubt about what We have revealed upon the tongue of our Prophet to you...' to the end of the *ayat*. This opinion is corroborated by the *verse,* ﴾*Say, [O Messenger of Allah], "O people, if you are in doubt as to my religion..."*﴿ [Surah Yunus 10:104]

---

lawful amount of wives allowed in the law.

Ostensibly Commiting a Sin

﴿ وَإِنْ كَانَ كَبُرَ عَلَيْكَ إِعْرَاضُهُمْ فَإِنِ اسْتَطَعْتَ أَنْ تَبْتَغِيَ نَفَقًا فِي الْأَرْضِ، أَوْ سُلَّمًا فِي السَّمَاءِ فَتَأْتِيَهُمْ بِآيَةٍ، وَلَوْ شَاءَ اللهُ لَجَمَعَهُمْ عَلَى الْهُدَى، فَلَا تَكُونَنَّ مِنَ الْجَاهِلِينَ ﴾

﴿And if their aversion is difficult for you, then if you are able to seek a tunnel into the earth or a stairway into the sky to bring them a sign, [then do so]. But if Allah had willed, He would have united them upon guidance. So never be of the ignorant.﴾

[Surah An'ām 6:35]

This verse does not contain anything that suggests that the Messenger ﷺ committed a sin for which Allah Most High had to rebuke him. The most that this verse could imply is Allah's desiring to lighten the grief that the polytheists' rejection was having on him ﷺ and to expose the reality of their souls to him. So had the Messenger of Allah ﷺ come to them with every single miracle, they would still not believe until they came face to face with the painful punishment.

Ibn 'Abbās ؓ said, 'At all times, the Messenger of Allah ﷺ was avid for all mankind to believe and follow him in guidance. So Allah informed him that none will believe in your invitation save the one who was previously decreed by Allah to be felicitous in the First Reminder (*dhikr al-ūlā*).'

About this, Allah Most High said at the end of this verse,

﴿ إِنَّمَا يَسْتَجِيبُ الَّذِينَ يَسْمَعُونَ وَالْمَوْتَى يَبْعَثُهُمُ اللَّهُ ثُمَّ إِلَيْهِ يُرْجَعُونَ ﴾

﴿Only those who hear will respond. But the deceased - Allah will resurrect them; then to Him they will be returned.﴾

[Surah An'ām 6:36]

The *deceased* here refers to the disbelievers who do not believe and do not respond to the invitation of truth.

And the proofs of his tremendous avidness ﷺ for his Community to embrace Islam within these verses is not hidden. Were he ﷺ able to bring a sign to them from under the earth or from the skies, he would have done so out of compassion for them and hoping for their faith (*īmān*). So Allah spoke the truth when He said:

﴿ لَقَدْ جَاءَكُمْ رَسُولٌ مِّنْ أَنفُسِكُمْ عَزِيزٌ عَلَيْهِ مَا عَنِتُّمْ حَرِيصٌ عَلَيْكُم بِالْمُؤْمِنِينَ رَءُوفٌ رَّحِيمٌ ﴾

﴿*There has certainly come to you a Messenger from among yourselves. Grievous to him is what you suffer; he is deeply concerned for you and to the believers is kind and merciful.*﴾

[Surah Tawba 9:128]

The Prophet ﷺ Ostensibly Expelling His Companions

﴿ وَلَا تَطْرُدِ الَّذِينَ يَدْعُونَ رَبَّهُم بِالْغَدَاةِ وَالْعَشِيِّ يُرِيدُونَ وَجْهَهُ ۖ مَا عَلَيْكَ مِنْ حِسَابِهِم مِّن شَيْءٍ وَمَا مِنْ حِسَابِكَ عَلَيْهِم مِّن شَيْءٍ فَتَطْرُدَهُمْ فَتَكُونَ مِنَ الظَّالِمِينَ ﴾

❮And do not send away those who call upon their Lord morning and afternoon, seeking His countenance. Not upon you is anything of their account and not upon them is anything of your account. So were you to send them away, you would [then] be of the wrongdoers❯

[Surah An'ām 6:52]

In this verse is a word of caution for the Messenger ﷺ in responding to the request of the disbelievers of Quraysh in expelling the disenfranchised believers. There is nothing therein that suggests he ﷺ actually expelled them. In fact, the Prophet ﷺ did nothing but restate the proposal of the polytheists [to expel the weak believers which] they presented to him. Thereafter, Allah's appraisal and warning came for restating it.

Ibn Jarīr ؓ reported that Ibn Mas'ud ؓ said: "The elite of Quraysh passed by the Messenger of Allah ﷺ and with him were Suhayb, Bilal, 'Ammar, Khabbab ؓ and others among the weak and disenfranchised Muslims. So the Quraysh said: "O Muhammad, are you pleased with these people [as Companions] from among your Community? Are these the people that Allah has favoured among us? Should we start to follow *these people*? Expel them; maybe if you expel them we will follow you." At that juncture, Allah revealed the following verse:

﴿ وَلَا تَطْرُدِ الَّذِينَ يَدْعُونَ رَبَّهُم بِالْغَدَاةِ وَالْعَشِيِّ ﴾

❮And do not send away those who call upon their Lord morning and afternoon...❯

[Surah An'ām 6:52]

If you understand this, it would become clear to you that the Messenger ﷺ did not expel those disenfranchised Companions. He only hypothetically considered distancing them from his gathering when the elite polytheists came to him, so that he could win their hearts to encourage them to believe. So Allah Most High prohibited carrying out that hypothetical consideration and commanded him ﷺ to make those poor, disenfranchised Companions the ones he ﷺ sits with and his intimate friends. This is corroborated by what Allah Most High said in surah al-Kahf:

﴿وَاصْبِرْ نَفْسَكَ مَعَ الَّذِينَ يَدْعُونَ رَبَّهُم بِالْغَدَاةِ وَالْعَشِيِّ يُرِيدُونَ وَجْهَهُ ۖ وَلَا تَعْدُ
عَيْنَاكَ عَنْهُمْ تُرِيدُ زِينَةَ الْحَيَاةِ الدُّنْيَا ۖ وَلَا تُطِعْ مَنْ أَغْفَلْنَا قَلْبَهُ عَن ذِكْرِنَا وَاتَّبَعَ هَوَاهُ
وَكَانَ أَمْرُهُ فُرُطًا﴾

﴿And keep yourself patient [by being] with those who call upon their Lord in the morning and the evening, seeking His countenance. And let not your eyes pass beyond them, desiring adornments of the worldly life, and do not obey one whose heart We have made heedless of Our remembrance and who follows his desire and whose affair is ever [in] neglect.﴾

[Surah Kahf 18:28]

The Ostensible 'Sin' of the Prophet

﴿إِنَّا فَتَحْنَا لَكَ فَتْحًا مُبِينًا. لِيَغْفِرَ لَكَ اللَّهُ مَا تَقَدَّمَ مِن ذَنبِكَ وَمَا تَأَخَّرَ﴾

❬Indeed, We have given you, [O Prophet], a clear victory. That Allah may forgive for you what preceded of your sin and what will follow and complete His favour upon you and guide you to a straight path.❭

[Surah Fatḥ 48:1-2]

Ibn Kathīr said,

> What is meant by the words of Allah Most High: ❬Indeed, We have given you, [O Messenger of Allah], a clear victory...❭ to the end of the verse is the Treaty of *Hudaybīyah*. Indeed because of it, an immense good resulted, people became safe, people were brought together, the believer began to speak to the disbeliever, and beneficial knowledge and faith began to spread.

Ibn al-Qayyim said:

> The treaty of *Hudaybīyah* was the pre-cursor and the ground-breaking first steps to this magnificent victory. People started to feel safe because of it, began speaking to each other, and began to dialogue about Islam. It afforded those Muslims who were suppressed in Mecca to openly practice their way of life, to invite others to it, to debate others about it with proofs, and multitudes entered Islam because of it. So because of all this, Allah called it a 'victory'.

As for the 'sin' mentioned in this verse, what is meant by it is performing something virtuous instead of something more virtuous and more preferred. Abū al-Saʿūd said in his *tafsir* of the words of Allah Most High:

﴿مَا تَقَدَّمَ مِن ذَنبِكَ وَمَا تَأَخَّرَ﴾

❬...what preceded of your sins and what will follow...❭

[Surah Fatḥ 48:2]

This refers to any opportunities that you have inadvertently missed related to leaving a preferred act. It was only called a 'sin' because of the Prophet's high rank.

In the book *Tafsir al-Wāḍiḥ* the following appears:

> The verse ❬...what preceded of your sins and what will follow...❭ [Surah

> Fatḥ 48:2] refers to any opportunity that the Prophet ﷺ missed to perform a more virtuous act [while opting to perform a less virtuous act]. Keeping in mind that he is divinely protected from disobeying his Lord, it is due to his ﷺ unparalleled rank [with Allah] that this was termed 'a sin.' This is in light of the principle that we quoted earlier: *hasanat al-abrar, sayyi'at al-muqarrabin* or 'the good deeds of the pious are the evil deeds of those brought close to Allah.'

It is also said that this refers to 'what he ﷺ deems to be a sin according to the high standards he set for himself [out of love for Allah], even if in reality, that was not the actual standard.' So it is plausible that the possessive-construct of the words in Allah's word ﴾*...your sin...*﴿ corroborates this meaning [i.e. something you consider to be a sin].

The Prophet's Ostensibly Concealing Love for Zaynab

﴿وَإِذْ تَقُولُ لِلَّذِي أَنْعَمَ اللَّهُ عَلَيْهِ وَأَنْعَمْتَ عَلَيْهِ أَمْسِكْ عَلَيْكَ زَوْجَكَ وَاتَّقِ اللَّهَ وَتُخْفِي فِي نَفْسِكَ مَا اللَّهُ مُبْدِيهِ وَتَخْشَى النَّاسَ وَاللَّهُ أَحَقُّ أَنْ تَخْشَاهُ﴾

﴿And remember, O Messenger of Allah], when you said to the one on whom Allah bestowed favour and on whom you bestowed favour, "Keep your wife and fear Allah," while you concealed within yourself that which Allah is to disclose. And you feared the people, while Allah has more right that you fear Him. So when Zayd had no longer any need for her, We married her to you in order that there not be upon the believers any discomfort concerning the wives of their adopted sons when they no longer have need of them. And ever is the command of Allah accomplished.﴾

[Surah Aḥzāb 33:37]

Here, some individuals with weak *īmān* and spiritually diseased hearts find it amusing to stir up doubts about the marriage of the Prophet ﷺ to Zaynab ﵂, who was previously married to his freed slave and foster son, Zayd b. Ḥārith ﵁, and to create a commotion about the Prophet's infallibility.

The Incorrect Interpretation

They claim that Prophet Muhammad ﷺ saw Zaynab, fell in love with her, and concealed this love. Then later on, he manifested it and desired to marry Zaynab, had her divorce her husband Zayd, then married her himself. They allege that the censure in this verse is because the Messenger ﷺ concealed his love for Zaynab ﵂.

Still others invented more lies and alleged that the Prophet ﷺ passed by the house of Zayd ﵁ while he was not at home, saw Zaynab ﵂, and something came into his heart and he said: "Glory be to the Turner of hearts!" Then, Zaynab heard the glorification of Allah and related it to Zayd. Zayd felt in his heart that he should divorce her so that the Messenger ﷺ could marry her.

There are actually other false allegations which the orientalists and those who resemble them among Muslims cling to. They allow themselves to plunge into disparaging the integrity of others and speaking about the Noble Prophet ﷺ, and they present an image of him that the average person will deem to be below common decency. Their chain of narrations for this are from some Judeo-Christian reports which have been inserted in books of *tafsir*. They are untrue narrations which have no validity whatsoever, as Abu Bakr b. al-ʿArabī ﷺ said.

The Correct Interpretation

The actual details of this topic are transmitted by Ibn Hātim via al-Suddī with the wording:

> It has reached us that this verse was revealed about Zaynab bint Jaḥsh ﷺ. Her mother was 'Umayyah bint ʿAbd al-Muṭṭalib, the maternal aunt of the Messenger of Allah ﷺ. The Messenger of Allah ﷺ wanted Zayd b. Ḥārithah, his free-slave, to marry her, but she was not in favour of it. Later, she had a change of heart and was pleased with what the Messenger of Allah arranged, so he got her married to Zayd. Thereafter, Allah ﷻ informed his Prophet ﷺ that Zaynab will be one of his wives. But he ﷺ felt reluctant and shy to instruct Zayd to divorce her. He continued to be pleasant and to socialize in goodness with Zayd and Zaynab whenever they were with people. And the Messenger of Allah ﷺ even instructed him to keep to his wife and fear Allah. He ﷺ feared that people would ridicule him and would say 'He married a woman who was previously married to his son.' About this incident, Allah Most High revealed:
>
> ﴿ وَمَا كَانَ لِمُؤْمِنٍ وَلَا مُؤْمِنَةٍ إِذَا قَضَى اللَّهُ وَرَسُولُهُ أَمْرًا أَن يَكُونَ لَهُمُ الْخِيَرَةُ مِنْ أَمْرِهِمْ ﴾
>
> ﴾*It is not for a believing man or a believing woman, when Allah and His Messenger have decided a matter, that they should [thereafter] have any choice about their affair.*﴿
>
> [Surah Aḥzāb 33:36]

It is narrated that ʿAlī b. al-Ḥusayn ﷺ said: "Allah informed His Prophet ﷺ that Zaynab ﷺ will be one of his wives *before* he himself married her. So when Zayd came to him complaining about her, the Prophet ﷺ said to him, 'Fear Allah and hold to your wife.' Allah rebuked him and said to him: 'I informed you that I will marry you to her and you conceal what you know; Allah will manifest it.'

So what the Messenger of Allah ﷺ concealed was not his love for Zaynab like the fabricators allege. He ﷺ did not conceal anything other than what Allah revealed to him about his [future] marriage to her out of an immense wisdom, which was to invalidate the Arabian Pre-Islamic system of adoption (*tabannī*).[20] The Messenger ﷺ feared that the hypocrites would say, '*Muhammad married his son's ex-wife,*' since Zayd ؓ was known as Zayd, son of Muhammad.

Shaykh al-Ḥijāzī ؒ says in his *Tafsir al-Wāḍiḥ*:

> One of the unfortunate things that detract from some of the books of *tafsir* is that some [incorrect] opinions are ascribed to senior scholars, while Allah knows very well that they are exonerated from that. Or they are in reality, noxious Judaeo-Christian reports that have been inserted, with either with good intentions or ill-will, by former Jews who embraced Islam. Of them is the *tafsir* of these verses related to issues that do not befit the average man, not to mention the best of creation ﷺ, about whom all people attest to his truthfulness and praiseworthy character ﷺ.

Even a cursory look at Zaynab's background ؓ and the circumstances of her marriage to Zayd ؓ would help us realize that their rocky relationship was nothing other than the obvious disparity in their respective ranks in society. Zaynab was a noble lady, whilst Zayd had been a slave. So Allah sought to test her with marriage to Zayd to abolish the zealous tribal customs and 'honour' of Pre-Islamic Arabian times, and to reframe the concept of honour to exclusively be found in submitting to Allah (Islam) and possessing *taqwa* or Godfearingness. So Zaynab voluntarily submitted with disinclination to the marriage [out of love for Allah] and submitted her body to Zayd, but not her soul. It was a source of emotional discomfort and constriction.

One should bear in mind that Prophet Muhammad ﷺ knew Zaynab ؓ from childhood because she was his paternal cousin, so who could prevent her from marrying him?[21] Furthermore, [looking at this situation

---

[20] In Arabic, the word *tabanni* (التبني) refers to changing the last name of the adoptee (i.e. family lineage). The Arabic word *haḍānah* or foster-care, which does not involve changing the adoptee's last name (i.e. family name) is extremely praiseworthy and encouraged in Islam. Hence, just as both *tabanni* and *ḥaḍānah* do not create actual blood ties, so too, 1) it does not create Islamically-legislated family inheritance, 2) it does not bypass gender-related rulings on covering (*hijab*) between the adoptee and the foster-family, and 3) nor does it allow the adoptee to assume the family name of the adopting family—except for purposes related to governmental identification and civil law. The adopted child *must be told* who his biological parents are, if they are known. Allah knows best.

[21] As marrying one's cousin was the normal custom at that time and remains lawful, although perhaps not recommended, to this day.

from a social studies perspective] why would a man [who loves a woman], suggest that that woman marry another man while she is a virgin, and he even conducts their marriage, she loses her virginity, and then after all that, turns around and desires her for marriage?

No, O People, think well about what you are saying and understand the truth in the correct context. Comprehend it and do not be misled or confused.

Look at what they are suggesting: 'What Muhammad was hiding was his love for Zaynab and *that* is why he was rebuked [in the Quran].'

But ask yourself: Is a man reprimanded because he did *not* proclaim his love for another man's wife?

No, the truth is that this marriage was a test for Zaynab and her husband from the very beginning. In the end, it was also a burdensome test for the Prophet ﷺ, because Allah had commanded him to marry her while knowing the consequences and tremendous stigma he would receive from society; Zaynab was formerly wedded to his freed slave Zayd. But the wisdom behind that, as the Quran articulates, was to eradicate the tribal custom that was practiced and widespread amongst the Arabs which was: '*The prohibition of marrying the foster-son's ex-wife*,' similar to the prohibition of marrying the ex-wife of one's biological son. The Quran attests:

﴿ لِكَيْ لَا يَكُونَ عَلَى الْمُؤْمِنِينَ حَرَجٌ فِي أَزْوَاجِ أَدْعِيَائِهِمْ إِذَا قَضَوْا مِنْهُنَّ وَطَرًا ۚ وَكَانَ أَمْرُ اللَّهِ مَفْعُولًا ﴾

﴾*...in order that there not be upon the believers any discomfort concerning the wives of their adopted sons when they no longer have need of them. And ever is the command of Allah accomplished.*﴿

[Surah Aḥzāb 33:37]

So what the Prophet ﷺ concealed in himself was his being upset with the result of the marriage [while remaining pleasant and social with them], his being hesitant in fulfilling the command of Allah regarding it [for fear of upsetting the couple], and his fear of the stigma and uproar in society—especially from the hypocrites when they would discover that the system of adoption which they founded has now been abolished. It is only for this reason that he ﷺ was rebuked.

I declare that the verse is explicit about this. It states that Allah will bring to light that which the Messenger ﷺ hid ﴾*...while you concealed within yourself that which Allah is to disclose*﴿ [Surah Ahzāb 33:37]. So what exactly did Allah bring to light, you ask? Did Allah bring to light the love of the Messenger for Zaynab? How ludicrous! The only thing Allah brought to light here is that the Messenger ﷺ [already knew that Zaynab was going to be his wife and] wanted to marry her *because Allah had already revealed to him that she will be his wife.* That is why Allah ﷻ explicitly mentioned in the following verse that He is the Arranger of this marriage between the Prophet ﷺ and Zaynab saying ﴿*...We married her to you...*﴾, and it is simply this foreknowledge that the Messenger concealed in himself. Allah declared:

﴿ فَلَمَّا قَضَىٰ زَيْدٌ مِنْهَا وَطَرًا زَوَّجْنَاكَهَا ﴾

﴿*So when Zayd had no longer any need for her, We married her to you...*﴾

[Surah Aḥzāb 33:37]

Thus, the claims of the fabricators are invalidated in front of irrefutable proof and clear evidences which demonstrate the infallibility of the Master of the Messengers, may Allah bless him and his family, and grant him His choicest benedictions and abundant peace. And all praise belongs to Allah, the Lord of the worlds.

Appendix on Prophet Dawud ﷺ and the Two Litigants

An excerpt from Imam al-Sabuni's Safwat al-tafasīr: Tafsir of Surah S'ad (38:21-24)

Some of the exegetes of Quran have made erroneous mistakes by transmitting some fabricated stories in their respective *tafsirs* that are based upon stories from the People of the Book (*Ahl al-Kitab*) without proper verification and investigation, that do not have a sound chain of narration (*sanad*), and that are impermissible to be relied upon. This is because they are from the Judeo-Christian stories (*Isra'īliyyat*) that negate Islam's creed (*'aqidah*) of the infallibility of the Prophets ﷺ and the myths that have crept into Islamic literature. The following will explain two false stories attributed to Prophet Dawud ﷺ that stand in contradistinction to the infallibility of the Prophets ﷺ.

False Stories Concerning Prophet Dawud ﷺ, General Uriah, and his Wife

The first example is what was falsely narrated about our master Dawud's ﷺ love for the wife of his army's leader named Uriah. Its summary is:

> *That Dawud ﷺ was walking along the roof of his abode and he saw a woman bathing. She caught his eye and he started to like her. She was the wife of one of his army generals named Uriah. Dawud wanted to get rid of her husband so he could marry her. So, he dispatched him to one of the battles, made him carry the banner (of war), and ordered him to attack and he was victorious. He sent the man out again and again to get rid of him until he was killed and then he married her...*

Hafiz Ibn Kathīr al-Shafi'i ﷺ said:

> Indeed, many of the *mufassirun* have mentioned here stories and reports, most of which are *Isra'ilīyyat*. Most of them are false and insidious.

We have intentionally not conveyed it in our book (*Ṣafwat al-tafāsīr*), sufficing with sheer mention of the story from the Holy Quran, and

Allah guides whoever He wills to the straight path.

Two Statements of the Pious Predecessors (Salaf) about this Incident

Imam Bayḍāwī ﵀ said:

> Regarding what was said *'That Dawud ﵇ sent Uriah several times to war, and ordered him to attack until he was killed. Then Dawud ﵇ married her'* – is a blatant lie and is fabricated.'

That is why Ali ﵁ said:

> Whoever speaks about what was falsely attributed to Dawud ﵇ by the 'storytellers' will be whipped 160 times, and this is the punishment for slandering the prophets ﵈.

What is the Correct Understanding of the Quranic Story of the Two Litigants?

Regarding this incident, what the Imams of *Tafsir* and the eminent scholars have said in explaining this incident is correct. Namely, that Dawud ﵇ would designate some of his time to discharge the affairs of the kingdom, to judge between people, other times for himself, and other times for worship (*'ibādah*) and recitation (*tartīl*) of the *Zabūr* (Psalms) to glorify Allah in his prayer niche (*miḥrāb*). If he entered into his *miḥrāb* for worship and seclusion (*khalwa*), then no one would bother him by entering upon him until he himself came out to the people.

One day, he was surprised by two men scaling the wall of the *miḥrāb* he would worship in. He became alarmed by them and entertained the thought of attacking the two men [in defence of their attack]. They immediately assured him they were two litigants who were disputing over an issue between them. So, one began speaking and put forth his dispute – like the Holy Quran stated in its clear verse:

﴿إِنَّ هَٰذَا أَخِي لَهُ تِسْعٌ وَتِسْعُونَ نَعْجَةً وَلِيَ نَعْجَةٌ وَاحِدَةٌ فَقَالَ أَكْفِلْنِيهَا وَعَزَّنِي فِي الْخِطَابِ﴾

Surely this is my brother; he has ninety-nine ewes and I have a single ewe; but he said: Make it over to me, and he has prevailed against me in discourse.

[Surah Sad:38-23)

And the way the case was presented by one of the litigants, he sensationalized it to seem that his brother was extremely oppressive to him and that it could not possibly be interpreted any other way. So in this way, Dawud عليه السلام was influenced to rule in favour of this man whom he heard this oppressive and shocking story from, and he did not even turn to the other man, seek an explanation from him, nor hear an argument from him. Rather, he immediately judged with his words (recorded in the Quran):

قَالَ لَقَدْ ظَلَمَكَ بِسُؤَالِ نَعْجَتِكَ إِلَىٰ نِعَاجِهِ ۖ

He (Dawud عليه السلام) said: 'Indeed he has oppressed you by asking you for your sheep...'

So Allah disciplined him for that and alerted him to the necessity of a judge (*qāḍī*) to ensure to establish the truth in his judgment and to hear the other disputant's side of the story.

﴿وَإِنَّ كَثِيرًا مِّنَ الْخُلَطَاءِ لَيَبْغِي بَعْضُهُمْ عَلَىٰ بَعْضٍ إِلَّا الَّذِينَ آمَنُوا وَعَمِلُوا
الصَّالِحَاتِ وَقَلِيلٌ مَّا هُمْ ۗ وَظَنَّ دَاوُودُ أَنَّمَا فَتَنَّاهُ فَاسْتَغْفَرَ رَبَّهُ وَخَرَّ رَاكِعًا وَأَنَابَ﴾

And indeed, many associates oppress one another, except for those who believe and do righteous deeds - and few are they." <u>And David became certain that We had tried him</u> [i.e. by testing to see if he would judge without listening to both sides], and he asked forgiveness of his Lord and fell down bowing [in prostration] and turned in repentance [to Allah].

[Surah Sad:38-24)

As for some of the other things that others have claimed, relying on some *Isra'īlīyāt* narrations—which we have previously discussed and cautioned against—indeed it does not even befit the ignorant sinners, much less the average Muslim. So how can we go ahead and attribute such labels to the Noble Prophets عليهم السلام? Nay, the choicest of prophets, Prophet Muhammad ﷺ? So, let whoever has a sound intellect and strong religious practice (*din*) think long and hard about this.

Index of Quranic Verses

General praise for the Prophets

1. Surah al-‘An ʿām 6:90

﴿أُولَئِكَ الَّذِينَ هَدَى اللَّهُ فَبِهُدَاهُمُ اقْتَدِهْ..﴾

﴿Those were the (prophets) who received Allah's guidance: Emulate the guidance they received.﴾

2. Surah al-Aḥzāb 33:21

﴿لَّقَدْ كَانَ لَكُمْ فِي رَسُولِ اللَّهِ أُسْوَةٌ حَسَنَةٌ..﴾

﴿Ye have indeed in the Messenger of Allah a beautiful pattern (of conduct).﴾

Isma

3. Surah Hūd 11:43

﴿قَالَ سَآوِي إِلَىٰ جَبَلٍ يَعْصِمُنِي مِنَ الْمَاءِ﴾

﴿But he said, "I will take refuge on a mountain to protect me (ya ʿṣimunī) from the water."﴾

4. Surah Yūsuf 12:32

﴿وَلَقَدْ رَاوَدتُّهُ عَن نَّفْسِهِ فَاسْتَعْصَمَ﴾

﴿And I certainly sought to seduce him, but he firmly refused (ʿfa ʿtaṣama).﴾

Special care before prophethood

5. Surah Taha 20:39

﴿ وَلِتُصْنَعَ عَلَى عَيْنِي﴾

﴿ ... that you would be brought up under My special care. ﴾

6. Surah Ṣād 38:47

﴿وَإِنَّهُمْ عِنْدَنَا لَمِنَ الْمُصْطَفَيْنَ الْأَخْيَارِ﴾

﴿And indeed they are, to Us, among the elect and outstanding.﴾

Divine Hifz

7. Surah Ḥadīd 57:28

﴿ يَا أَيُّهَا الَّذِينَ آمَنُوا اتَّقُوا اللَّهَ وَآمِنُوا بِرَسُولِهِ يُؤْتِكُمْ كِفْلَيْنِ مِن رَّحْمَتِهِ وَيَجْعَل لَّكُمْ نُورًا
تَمْشُونَ بِهِ وَيَغْفِرْ لَكُمْ ۚ وَاللَّهُ غَفُورٌ رَّحِيمٌ ﴾

﴿O you who have believed! Fear Allah and believe in His Messenger; He will then give you a double portion of His mercy and make for you a light by which you will walk and forgive you; and Allah is Forgiving and Merciful.﴾

8.Surah Anbiyā' 21:73

﴿وَجَعَلْنَاهُمْ أَئِمَّةً يَهْدُونَ بِأَمْرِنَا وَأَوْحَيْنَا إِلَيْهِمْ فِعْلَ الْخَيْرَاتِ وَإِقَامَ الصَّلَاةِ وَإِيتَاءَ الزَّكَاةِ ۖ
وَكَانُوا لَنَا عَابِدِينَ﴾

﴿And We made them leaders, guiding by Our Command, and We sent them inspiration to do good deeds, to establish regular prayers, and to practise regular charity; and they constantly served Us.﴾

9. Surah Ṭāhā 20:121

﴿وَعَصَىٰ آدَمُ رَبَّهُ فَغَوَىٰ﴾

﴿And Adam 'disobeyed' his Lord and erred. ﴾

10. Surah Hūd 11:46

﴿إِنِّي أَعِظُكَ أَن تَكُونَ مِنَ الْجَاهِلِينَ﴾

﴾Indeed, I advise you, lest you be among the ignorant.﴿

11. Surah Fatḥ 48:2

﴿ لِّيَغْفِرَ لَكَ اللَّهُ مَا تَقَدَّمَ مِن ذَنبِكَ.. ﴾

﴾That Allah may forgive for you what preceded of your sin and what will follow.﴿

12. Surah An ʿam 6:90

﴿أُولَٰئِكَ الَّذِينَ هَدَى اللَّهُ فَبِهُدَاهُمُ اقْتَدِهْ قُل لَّا أَسْأَلُكُمْ عَلَيْهِ أَجْرًا إِنْ هُوَ إِلَّا ذِكْرَىٰ لِلْعَالَمِينَ﴾

﴾Those are the ones whom Allah has guided, so from their guidance take an example. Say, "I ask of you for this message no payment. It is not but a reminder for the worlds."﴿

13. Surah Anbiyā' 21:73

﴿وَجَعَلْنَاهُمْ أَئِمَّةً يَهْدُونَ بِأَمْرِنَا وَأَوْحَيْنَا إِلَيْهِمْ فِعْلَ الْخَيْرَاتِ وَإِقَامَ الصَّلَاةِ وَإِيتَاءَ الزَّكَاةِ ۖ
وَكَانُوا لَنَا عَابِدِينَ﴾

﴾And We made them leaders guiding by Our command. We inspired to them the doing of good deeds, establishment of prayer, and giving of zakah; and they were worshippers of Us.﴿

14. Surah Ṭāhā 20:121-122

﴿فَأَكَلَا مِنْهَا فَبَدَتْ لَهُمَا سَوْآتُهُمَا وَطَفِقَا يَخْصِفَانِ عَلَيْهِمَا مِن وَرَقِ الْجَنَّةِ ۚ وَعَصَىٰ آدَمُ رَبَّهُ
فَغَوَىٰ ﴿١٢١﴾ ثُمَّ اجْتَبَاهُ رَبُّهُ فَتَابَ عَلَيْهِ وَهَدَىٰ﴾

﴾And Adam and his wife ate of it, and their private parts became apparent to them, and they began to fasten over themselves from the leaves of Paradise. Adam disobeyed his Lord and erred. Then his Lord chose him and turned to him in forgiveness and guided him.﴿

﴾Then his Lord selected him.﴿

15. Surah Ṭāhā 20:115

﴿وَلَقَدْ عَهِدْنَا إِلَىٰ آدَمَ مِن قَبْلُ فَنَسِيَ وَلَمْ نَجِدْ لَهُ عَزْمًا﴾

﴾ We had already taken a promise from Adam before, but he forgot; and We found not in him determination.﴿

16. Surah Baqara 2:35

﴿ وَلَا تَقْرَبَا هَٰذِهِ الشَّجَرَةَ﴾

﴾...do not approach this tree...﴿

17. Surah Baqara 2:286

﴿رَبَّنَا لَا تُؤَاخِذْنَا إِن نَّسِينَا أَوْ أَخْطَأْنَا﴾

﴾ Our Lord, do not impose blame upon us if we have forgotten or erred.﴿

18. Surah Ṭāhā 20:115

﴿ فَنَسِيَ وَلَمْ نَجِدْ لَهُ عَزْمًا﴾

﴾...but he forgot; and We found not in him determination.﴿

19. Surah Ṭāhā 20:121

﴿ وَعَصَىٰ آدَمُ رَبَّهُ فَغَوَىٰ ﴾

﴾And Adam disobeyed his Lord.﴿

2o. Surah Baqara 2:35

﴿فَتَكُونَا مِنَ الظَّالِمِينَ﴾

﴾...lest you be among the wrongdoers.﴿

21. Surah Ṭāhā 20:122

﴿ثُمَّ اجْتَبَاهُ رَبُّهُ فَتَابَ عَلَيْهِ وَهَدَىٰ﴾

﴾ Then his Lord chose him and turned to him in forgiveness

and guided him!﴾

22. Surah ʿAn ʿām 6:76-79

﴿ فَلَمَّا جَنَّ عَلَيْهِ اللَّيْلُ رَأَىٰ كَوْكَبًا ۖ قَالَ هَٰذَا رَبِّي ۖ فَلَمَّا أَفَلَ قَالَ لَا أُحِبُّ الْآفِلِينَ ﴿٦٧﴾
فَلَمَّا رَأَى الْقَمَرَ بَازِغًا قَالَ هَٰذَا رَبِّي ۖ فَلَمَّا أَفَلَ قَالَ لَئِن لَّمْ يَهْدِنِي رَبِّي لَأَكُونَنَّ مِنَ الْقَوْمِ
الضَّالِّينَ ﴿٧٧﴾ فَلَمَّا رَأَى الشَّمْسَ بَازِغَةً قَالَ هَٰذَا رَبِّي هَٰذَا أَكْبَرُ ۖ فَلَمَّا أَفَلَتْ قَالَ يَا قَوْمِ إِنِّي
بَرِيءٌ مِّمَّا تُشْرِكُونَ ﴿٨٧﴾ إِنِّي وَجَّهْتُ وَجْهِيَ لِلَّذِي فَطَرَ السَّمَاوَاتِ وَالْأَرْضَ حَنِيفًا ۖ
وَمَا أَنَا مِنَ الْمُشْرِكِينَ ﴾

﴿Thus when the night covered him [with darkness], he saw a star. He said, "This is my lord." But when it set, he said, "I like not those that disappear." And when he saw the moon rising, he said, "This is my lord." But when it set, he said, "Unless my Lord guides me, I will surely be among the people gone astray." And when he saw the sun rising, he said, "This is my lord; this is greater." But when it set, he said, "O my people, indeed I am free from what you associate with Allah. Indeed, I have turned my face toward He who created the heavens and the earth, inclining toward truth, and I am not of those who associate others with Allah." ﴾

23. Surah ʿAn ʿām 6:74-76

﴿ وَإِذْ قَالَ إِبْرَاهِيمُ لِأَبِيهِ آزَرَ أَتَتَّخِذُ أَصْنَامًا آلِهَةً ۖ إِنِّي أَرَاكَ وَقَوْمَكَ فِي ضَلَالٍ مُّبِينٍ ﴿٤٧﴾
وَكَذَٰلِكَ نُرِي إِبْرَاهِيمَ مَلَكُوتَ السَّمَاوَاتِ وَالْأَرْضِ وَلِيَكُونَ مِنَ الْمُوقِنِينَ ﴿٥٧﴾ فَلَمَّا جَنَّ عَلَيْهِ
اللَّيْلُ رَأَىٰ كَوْكَبًا.. ﴾

﴿And [mention, O Muhammad], when Ibrahim said to his father Azar, "Do you take idols as deities?" Indeed, I see you and your people to be in manifest error.﴾ ﴿ And thus did We show Ibrahim the realm of the heavens and the earth that he would be among the certain in faith.﴾ ﴿ So when the night covered him with darkness, he saw a star﴾

24. Surah ʿAn ʿām 6:75

﴿ وَكَذَٰلِكَ نُرِي إِبْرَاهِيمَ مَلَكُوتَ السَّمَاوَاتِ وَالْأَرْضِ وَلِيَكُونَ مِنَ الْمُوقِنِينَ ﴾

﴿And thus did We show Abraham the realm of the heavens and the earth that he would be among the certain in faith.﴾

25. Surah 'An'ām 6:83

﴿وَتِلْكَ حُجَّتُنَا آتَيْنَاهَا إِبْرَاهِيمَ عَلَىٰ قَوْمِهِ ۚ نَرْفَعُ دَرَجَاتٍ مَّن نَّشَاءُ ۗ إِنَّ رَبَّكَ حَكِيمٌ عَلِيمٌ﴾

﴿And that was Our conclusive argument which We gave Ibrahim against his people. We raise by degrees whom We will. Indeed, your Lord is Wise and Knowing.﴾

26. Surah 'An'ām 6:77

﴿لَئِن لَّمْ يَهْدِنِي رَبِّي لَأَكُونَنَّ مِنَ الْقَوْمِ الضَّالِّينَ﴾

﴿Unless my Lord guides me, I will surely be among the people gone astray.﴾

27. Surah 'An'ām 6:78-83]

﴿ قَالَ يَا قَوْمِ إِنِّي بَرِيءٌ مِّمَّا تُشْرِكُونَ ﴿٧٨﴾ إِنِّي وَجَّهْتُ وَجْهِيَ لِلَّذِي فَطَرَ السَّمَاوَاتِ
وَالْأَرْضَ حَنِيفًا ۖ وَمَا أَنَا مِنَ الْمُشْرِكِينَ ﴿٧٩﴾.. إلى قوله تبارك وتعالى ... وَتِلْكَ حُجَّتُنَا
آتَيْنَاهَا إِبْرَاهِيمَ عَلَىٰ قَوْمِهِ ۚ نَرْفَعُ دَرَجَاتٍ مَّن نَّشَاءُ ۗ إِنَّ رَبَّكَ حَكِيمٌ عَلِيمٌ﴾

﴿...O my people, indeed I am free from what you associate with Allah. Indeed, I have turned my face toward He who created the heavens and the earth, inclining toward truth, and I am not of those who associate others with Allah. And his people argued with him. He said, "Do you argue with me concerning Allah while He has guided me? And I fear not what you associate with Him [and will not be harmed] unless my Lord should will something. My Lord encompasses all things in knowledge; then will you not remember? And how should I fear what you associate while you do not fear that you have associated with Allah that for which He has not sent down to you any authority? So which of the two parties has more right to security, if you should know? They who believe and do not mix their belief with injustice - those will have security, and they are [rightly] guided. And that was Our conclusive argument which We gave Abraham against his people. We raise by degrees whom We will. Indeed, your Lord is Wise and Knowing.﴾

28. Surah 'Anbiyā' 21:51

﴿وَلَقَدْ آتَيْنَا إِبْرَاهِيمَ رُشْدَهُ مِن قَبْلُ وَكُنَّا بِهِ عَالِمِينَ﴾

﴿And We had certainly given Abraham his sound judgement before, and We were of him well-Knowing.﴿

29. Surah Baqara 2:260

﴿ وَإِذْ قَالَ إِبْرَاهِيمُ رَبِّ أَرِنِي كَيْفَ تُحْيِي الْمَوْتَىٰ ۖ قَالَ أَوَلَمْ تُؤْمِن ۖ قَالَ بَلَىٰ وَلَٰكِن لِّيَطْمَئِنَّ
قَلْبِي ۖ قَالَ فَخُذْ أَرْبَعَةً مِّنَ الطَّيْرِ فَصُرْهُنَّ إِلَيْكَ ثُمَّ اجْعَلْ عَلَىٰ كُلِّ جَبَلٍ مِّنْهُنَّ جُزْءًا ثُمَّ ادْعُهُنَّ
يَأْتِينَكَ سَعْيًا ۚ وَاعْلَمْ أَنَّ اللَّهَ عَزِيزٌ حَكِيمٌ ﴾

﴾And mention when Ibrahim said, "My Lord, show me how You give life to the dead." Allah said, "Have you not believed?" He said, "Yes, but I ask only that my heart may be satisfied." Allah said, "Take four birds and commit them to yourself. Then after slaughtering them put on each mountain a portion of them; then call them - they will come jogging] to you in haste." And know that Allah is Exalted in Might and Wise. ﴿

30. Surah Baqara 2:260

﴿وَإِذْ قَالَ إِبْرَاهِيمُ رَبِّ أَرِنِي كَيْفَ تُحْيِي الْمَوْتَىٰ﴾

﴾And mention when Abraham said, "My Lord, show me how You give life to the dead." ﴿

31. Surah Ḥujurāt 49:10

﴿إِنَّمَا الْمُؤْمِنُونَ إِخْوَةٌ ﴾

﴾The believers are but a fraternity.﴿

32. Surah Yūsuf 12:30-31

﴿ وَقَالَ نِسْوَةٌ فِي الْمَدِينَةِ امْرَأَتُ الْعَزِيزِ تُرَاوِدُ فَتَاهَا عَن نَّفْسِهِ ۖ قَدْ شَغَفَهَا حُبًّا ۖ إِنَّا
لَنَرَاهَا فِي ضَلَالٍ مُّبِينٍ ﴿٣٠﴾ فَلَمَّا سَمِعَتْ بِمَكْرِهِنَّ أَرْسَلَتْ إِلَيْهِنَّ وَأَعْتَدَتْ لَهُنَّ مُتَّكَأً وَآتَتْ
كُلَّ وَاحِدَةٍ مِّنْهُنَّ سِكِّينًا وَقَالَتِ اخْرُجْ عَلَيْهِنَّ ۖ فَلَمَّا رَأَيْنَهُ أَكْبَرْنَهُ وَقَطَّعْنَ أَيْدِيَهُنَّ وَقُلْنَ حَاشَ
لِلَّهِ مَا هَٰذَا بَشَرًا إِنْ هَٰذَا إِلَّا مَلَكٌ كَرِيمٌ ﴾

﴾And women in the city said, "The wife of the minister is seeking to seduce her slave boy; he has impassioned her with love. Indeed, we see her to be in clear error." So when she heard of their scheming, she sent for them and prepared for them a banquet and gave each one of them a knife and said to Joseph, "Come out before them." And when they saw him, they greatly admired him and cut their hands and said, "Perfect is Allah! This is not a man; this is none but a noble angel." ﴾

33. Surah Yūsuf 12:21

﴿وَقَالَ الَّذِي اشْتَرَاهُ مِن مِّصْرَ لِامْرَأَتِهِ أَكْرِمِي مَثْوَاهُ عَسَىٰ أَن يَنفَعَنَا أَوْ نَتَّخِذَهُ وَلَدًا﴾

﴿And the one from Egypt who bought him said to his wife, "Make his residence comfortable. Perhaps he will benefit us, or we will adopt him as a son." ﴾

34. Surah Yūsuf 12:24

﴿ وَلَقَدْ هَمَّتْ بِهِ ۖ وَهَمَّ بِهَا لَوْلَا أَن رَّأَىٰ بُرْهَانَ رَبِّهِ﴾

﴿And she was determined [to seduce] him, and he would have inclined to her had he not seen the proof of his Lord.﴾

35. Surah Yūsuf 12:26

﴿قَالَ هِيَ رَاوَدَتْنِي عَن نَّفْسِي﴾

﴿ Joseph said, "It was she who sought to seduce me.﴾

36. Surah Yūsuf 12:52

﴿ذَٰلِكَ لِيَعْلَمَ أَنِّي لَمْ أَخُنْهُ بِالْغَيْبِ﴾

﴿That is so the minister will know that I did not betray him in his absence...﴾

37. Surah Yūsuf 12:24

﴿كَذَٰلِكَ لِنَصْرِفَ عَنْهُ السُّوءَ وَالْفَحْشَاءَ﴾

﴿Thus it was that We should avert from him evil and immorality.﴾

38. Surah Yūsuf 12:23

﴿وَرَاوَدَتْهُ الَّتِي هُوَ فِي بَيْتِهَا عَن نَّفْسِهِ وَغَلَّقَتِ الْأَبْوَابَ وَقَالَتْ هَيْتَ لَكَ ۚ قَالَ مَعَاذَ اللَّهِ ۖ إِنَّهُ رَبِّي أَحْسَنَ مَثْوَايَ ۖ إِنَّهُ لَا يُفْلِحُ الظَّالِمُونَ﴾

﴿And she, in whose house he was, sought to seduce him. She closed the doors and said, "Come, you." He said, "[I seek] the refuge of Allah.

Indeed, he is my master, who has made good my residence." Indeed, wrongdoers will not succeed.﴿

39. Surah Yūsuf 12:23

﴿قَالَ مَعَاذَ اللَّهِ ۖ إِنَّهُ رَبِّي أَحْسَنَ مَثْوَايَ ۖ إِنَّهُ لَا يُفْلِحُ الظَّالِمُونَ﴾

﴾ He said, "[I seek] the refuge of Allah. Indeed, he is my master, who has made good my residence." ﴿

40. Surah Yūsuf 12:25

﴿ وَاسْتَبَقَا الْبَابَ وَقَدَّتْ قَمِيصَهُ مِن دُبُرٍ وَأَلْفَيَا سَيِّدَهَا لَدَى الْبَابِ ﴾

﴾And they both raced to the door, and she tore his shirt from the back, and they found her husband at the door.﴿

41. Surah Yūsuf 12:26-28

﴿ وَشَهِدَ شَاهِدٌ مِّنْ أَهْلِهَا إِن كَانَ قَمِيصُهُ قُدَّ مِن قُبُلٍ ﴾

﴾And a witness from her family testified. "If his shirt is torn from the front,﴿ i.e. it was rent from the front.

﴿فَصَدَقَتْ وَهُوَ مِنَ الْكَاذِبِينَ ﴿٢٦﴾ وَإِن كَانَ قَمِيصُهُ قُدَّ مِن دُبُرٍ ﴾

﴾...then she has told the truth, and he is of the liars. then she has told the truth, and he is of the liars. But if his shirt is torn from the back, i.e. it was torn from the back. ﴿

﴿ فَكَذَبَتْ وَهُوَ مِنَ الصَّادِقِينَ ﴿٧٢﴾ فَلَمَّا رَأَىٰ قَمِيصَهُ قُدَّ مِن دُبُرٍ قَالَ إِنَّهُ مِن كَيْدِكُنَّ ۖ إِنَّ كَيْدَكُنَّ عَظِيمٌ ﴾

﴾...then she has lied, and he is of the truthful. So when her husband saw his shirt torn from the back, he said, "Indeed, it is of the women's plan. Indeed, your plan is great." ﴿

42. Surah Yūsuf 12:33

﴿قَالَ رَبِّ السِّجْنُ أَحَبُّ إِلَيَّ مِمَّا يَدْعُونَنِي إِلَيْهِ ۖ وَإِلَّا تَصْرِفْ عَنِّي كَيْدَهُنَّ أَصْبُ إِلَيْهِنَّ وَأَكُن مِّنَ الْجَاهِلِينَ ﴾

﴾He said, "My Lord, prison is more to my liking than that to which they invite me. And if You do not avert from me their plan, I might incline toward them and thus be of the ignorant." ﴾

43. Surah Yūsuf 12:22-23

﴿وَلَمَّا بَلَغَ أَشُدَّهُ آتَيْنَاهُ حُكْمًا وَعِلْمًا وَكَذَٰلِكَ نَجْزِي الْمُحْسِنِينَ، وَرَاوَدَتْهُ الَّتِي هُوَ فِي بَيْتِهَا عَن نَّفْسِهِ﴾

﴿And when Joseph reached maturity, We gave him judgment and knowledge. Thus We reward the doers of good. And she, in whose house he was, sought to seduce him.﴾

44. Surah Yūsuf 12:31-32

﴿فَلَمَّا رَأَيْنَهُ أَكْبَرْنَهُ وَقَطَّعْنَ أَيْدِيَهُنَّ وَقُلْنَ حَاشَ لِلَّهِ مَا هَٰذَا بَشَرًا إِنْ هَٰذَا إِلَّا مَلَكٌ كَرِيمٌ ﴿٣١﴾ قَالَتْ فَذَٰلِكُنَّ الَّذِي لُمْتُنَّنِي فِيهِ ۖ وَلَقَدْ رَاوَدتُّهُ عَن نَّفْسِهِ فَاسْتَعْصَمَ﴾

﴿And when they saw him, they greatly admired him and cut their hands and said, "How perfect is Allah! This is not a man; this is none but a noble angel." She said, "That is the one about whom you blamed me. And I certainly sought to seduce him, but he firmly refused;"﴾

45. Surah Yūsuf 12:35

﴿ثُمَّ بَدَا لَهُم مِّن بَعْدِ مَا رَأَوُا الْآيَاتِ لَيَسْجُنُنَّهُ حَتَّىٰ حِينٍ﴾

﴿Then it appeared to them after they had seen the signs that the minister should surely imprison him for a time.﴾

46. Surah Yūsuf 12:34

﴿فَاسْتَجَابَ لَهُ رَبُّهُ فَصَرَفَ عَنْهُ كَيْدَهُنَّ ۚ إِنَّهُ هُوَ السَّمِيعُ الْعَلِيمُ﴾

﴿So his Lord responded to him and averted from him their plan. Indeed, He is the Hearing, the Knowing.﴾]

47. Surah Yūsuf 12:50

﴿وَقَالَ الْمَلِكُ ائْتُونِي بِهِ ۖ فَلَمَّا جَاءَهُ الرَّسُولُ قَالَ ارْجِعْ إِلَىٰ رَبِّكَ﴾

﴿And the king said, "Bring him to me." But when the messenger came to him, Joseph said, "Return to your master..."﴾

48. Surah Yūsuf 12:50

﴿فَاسْأَلْهُ مَا بَالُ النِّسْوَةِ اللَّاتِي قَطَّعْنَ أَيْدِيَهُنَّ ۚ إِنَّ رَبِّي بِكَيْدِهِنَّ عَلِيمٌ﴾

﴾...and ask him what is the case of the women who cut their hands. Indeed, my Lord is Knowing of their plan.﴿

49. Surah Yūsuf 12:51-52

﴿قَالَ مَا خَطْبُكُنَّ إِذْ رَاوَدتُّنَّ يُوسُفَ عَن نَّفْسِهِ ۚ قُلْنَ حَاشَ لِلَّهِ مَا عَلِمْنَا عَلَيْهِ مِن سُوءٍ ۚ قَالَتِ امْرَأَتُ الْعَزِيزِ الْآنَ حَصْحَصَ﴾

﴾ Said the king to the women, "What was your condition when you sought to seduce Joseph?" They said, "How perfect is Allah! We know about him no evil." The wife of the minister said, "Now the truth has become evident."(i.e. it is exposed and manifest.) ﴿

﴿الْحَقُّ أَنَا رَاوَدتُّهُ عَن نَّفْسِهِ وَإِنَّهُ لَمِنَ الصَّادِقِينَ ﴿٥١﴾ ذَٰلِكَ لِيَعْلَمَ أَنِّي لَمْ أَخُنْهُ بِالْغَيْبِ وَأَنَّ اللَّهَ لَا يَهْدِي كَيْدَ الْخَائِنِينَ﴾

﴾It was I who sought to seduce him, and indeed, he is of the truthful.﴿ ﴾That is so the minister will know that I did not betray him in his absence and that Allah does not guide the plan of the treacherous.﴿

50. Surah Hūd 11:45-46

﴿الر ۚ كِتَابٌ أُحْكِمَتْ آيَاتُهُ ثُمَّ فُصِّلَتْ مِن لَّدُنْ حَكِيمٍ خَبِيرٍ...قَالَ يَا نُوحُ إِنَّهُ لَيْسَ مِنْ أَهْلِكَ ۖ إِنَّهُ عَمَلٌ غَيْرُ صَالِحٍ ۖ فَلَا تَسْأَلْنِ مَا لَيْسَ لَكَ بِهِ عِلْمٌ ۖ إِنِّي أَعِظُكَ أَن تَكُونَ مِنَ الْجَاهِلِينَ﴾

﴾And Noah called to his Lord and said, "My Lord, indeed my son is of my family; and indeed, Your promise is true; and You are the most just of judges!﴿ ﴾ He said, "O Noah, indeed he is not of your family; indeed, he is one whose work was other than righteous, so ask Me not for that about which you have no knowledge. Indeed, I advise you, lest you be among the ignorant."﴿

51. Surah Hūd 11:37

﴿وَلَا تُخَاطِبْنِي فِي الَّذِينَ ظَلَمُوا ۚ إِنَّهُم مُّغْرَقُونَ﴾

﴾...and do not address Me concerning those who have wronged; indeed, they are to be drowned.﴿

52. Surah Nūḥ 11:46

﴿ لَيْسَ مِنْ أَهْلِكَ ﴾

﴿...indeed he is not of your family;﴾

53. Surah 'Anbiyā' 21:87-88

﴿ وَذَا النُّونِ إِذ ذَّهَبَ مُغَاضِبًا فَظَنَّ أَن لَّن نَّقْدِرَ عَلَيْهِ فَنَادَىٰ فِي الظُّلُمَاتِ أَن لَّا إِلَٰهَ إِلَّا أَنتَ
سُبْحَانَكَ إِنِّي كُنتُ مِنَ الظَّالِمِينَ فَاسْتَجَبْنَا لَهُ وَنَجَّيْنَاهُ مِنَ الْغَمِّ ۚ وَكَذَٰلِكَ نُنجِي الْمُؤْمِنِينَ﴾

﴿And [mention] the man of the fish, when he went off in anger and thought that We would not decree anything upon him. And he called out within the darknesses, "There is no deity except You; exalted are You. Indeed, I have been of the wrongdoers." So We responded to him and saved him from the distress. Thus do We save the believers.﴾

54. Surah 'Anbiyā' 21:87

﴿وَذَا النُّونِ إِذ ذَّهَبَ مُغَاضِبًا﴾

﴿And mention the man of the fish [Dhu-nūn], when he went off in anger.﴾

55. Surah Qalam 68:48-49

﴿فَاصْبِرْ لِحُكْمِ رَبِّكَ وَلَا تَكُن كَصَاحِبِ الْحُوتِ إِذْ نَادَىٰ وَهُوَ مَكْظُومٌ
وَلَا أَن تَدَارَكَهُ نِعْمَةٌ مِّن رَّبِّهِ لَنُبِذَ بِالْعَرَاءِ وَهُوَ مَذْمُومٌ. ﴿٩٤﴾ فَاجْتَبَاهُ رَبُّهُ فَجَعَلَهُ
مِنَ الصَّالِحِينَ﴾

﴿Then be patient for the decision of your Lord, [O Muhammad], and be not like the companion of the fish when he cried out while he was distressed. Were it not that a favor from his Lord overtook him, he would have been thrown onto the naked shore while he was censured. And his Lord chose him and made him of the righteous.﴾

56. Surah Fajr 89:16

﴿وَأَمَّا إِذَا مَا ابْتَلَاهُ فَقَدَرَ عَلَيْهِ رِزْقَهُ فَيَقُولُ رَبِّي أَهَانَنِ ﴾

﴿But when He tries him and constricts his provision, he says, "My Lord has humiliated me."﴾

57. Surah Anfāl 8:67-68

﴿مَا كَانَ لِنَبِيٍّ أَن يَكُونَ لَهُ أَسْرَىٰ حَتَّىٰ يُثْخِنَ فِي الْأَرْضِ ۚ تُرِيدُونَ عَرَضَ الدُّنْيَا وَاللَّهُ يُرِيدُ
الْآخِرَةَ ۗ وَاللَّهُ عَزِيزٌ حَكِيمٌ ﴿٧٦﴾ لَّوْلَا كِتَابٌ مِّنَ اللَّهِ سَبَقَ لَمَسَّكُمْ فِيمَا أَخَذْتُمْ
عَذَابٌ عَظِيمٌ﴾

﴾It is not for a prophet to have captives of war until he inflicts a massacre [upon Allah's enemies] in the land. Some Muslims desire the commodities of this world, but Allah desires for you the Hereafter. And Allah is Exalted in Might and Wise. If not for a decree from Allah that preceded, you would have been touched for what you took by a great punishment.﴿

58. Surah Tawba 9:43

﴿عَفَا اللَّهُ عَنكَ لِمَ أَذِنتَ لَهُمْ حَتَّىٰ يَتَبَيَّنَ لَكَ الَّذِينَ صَدَقُوا وَتَعْلَمَ الْكَاذِبِينَ﴾

﴾May Allah pardon you, [O Muhammad]; why did you give them permission to remain behind? [You should not have] until it was evident to you who were truthful and you knew who were the liars.﴿

59. Surah 'Abasa 80:1-4

﴿عَبَسَ وَتَوَلَّىٰ ﴿١﴾ أَن جَاءَهُ الْأَعْمَىٰ ﴿٢﴾ وَمَا يُدْرِيكَ لَعَلَّهُ يَزَّكَّىٰ ﴿٣﴾ أَوْ يَذَّكَّرُ فَتَنفَعَهُ
الذِّكْرَىٰ﴾

﴾He frowned and turned away. Because there came to him the blind man, [interrupting]. But what would make you perceive, [O Muhammad], that perhaps he might be purified. Or be reminded and the remembrance would benefit him?﴿

60. Surah Bani Israīl 17:73-76

﴿وَإِن كَادُوا لَيَفْتِنُونَكَ عَنِ الَّذِي أَوْحَيْنَا إِلَيْكَ لِتَفْتَرِيَ عَلَيْنَا غَيْرَهُ ۖ وَإِذًا لَّاتَّخَذُوكَ خَلِيلًا ﴿٣٧﴾
وَلَوْلَا أَن ثَبَّتْنَاكَ لَقَدْ كِدتَّ تَرْكَنُ إِلَيْهِمْ شَيْئًا قَلِيلًا ﴿٤٧﴾ إِذًا لَّأَذَقْنَاكَ ضِعْفَ الْحَيَاةِ وَضِعْفَ
الْمَمَاتِ ثُمَّ لَا تَجِدُ لَكَ عَلَيْنَا نَصِيرًا﴾

﴾And indeed, they were about to tempt you away from that which We revealed to you in order to make you invent about Us something else; and then they would have taken you as a friend. And if We had not strengthened you, you would have almost inclined to them a little﴿ ﴾Then if you had, We would have made you taste double punishment in life and double after death. Then you would not find for yourself against Us a helper.﴿

61. Surah Aḥzāb 33:1-2

﴿يَا أَيُّهَا النَّبِيُّ اتَّقِ اللَّهَ وَلَا تُطِعِ الْكَافِرِينَ وَالْمُنَافِقِينَ ۗ إِنَّ اللَّهَ كَانَ عَلِيمًا حَكِيمًا ﴿١﴾ وَاتَّبِعْ
مَا يُوحَىٰ إِلَيْكَ مِن رَّبِّكَ ۚ إِنَّ اللَّهَ كَانَ بِمَا تَعْمَلُونَ خَبِيرًا﴾

﴾O Prophet, fear Allah and do not obey the disbelievers and the hypocrites. Indeed, Allah is ever Knowing and Wise﴿ ﴾And follow that which is revealed to you from your Lord. Indeed Allah is, with what you do, well-Aware.﴿

62. Surah Yūnus 10:94

﴿فَإِن كُنتَ فِي شَكٍّ مِّمَّا أَنزَلْنَا إِلَيْكَ فَاسْأَلِ الَّذِينَ يَقْرَءُونَ الْكِتَابَ مِن قَبْلِكَ ۚ لَقَدْ جَاءَكَ الْحَقُّ
مِن رَّبِّكَ فَلَا تَكُونَنَّ مِنَ الْمُمْتَرِينَ﴾

﴾So if you are in doubt, [O Muhammad], about that which We have revealed to you, then ask those who have been reading the Scripture before you. The truth has certainly come to you from your Lord, so never be among the doubters.﴿

63. Surah An ʿām 6:35

﴿وَإِن كَانَ كَبُرَ عَلَيْكَ إِعْرَاضُهُمْ فَإِنِ اسْتَطَعْتَ أَن تَبْتَغِيَ نَفَقًا فِي الْأَرْضِ أَوْ سُلَّمًا فِي السَّمَاءِ
فَتَأْتِيَهُم بِآيَةٍ ۚ وَلَوْ شَاءَ اللَّهُ لَجَمَعَهُمْ عَلَى الْهُدَىٰ ۚ فَلَا تَكُونَنَّ مِنَ الْجَاهِلِينَ﴾

﴾And if their evasion is difficult for you, then if you are able to seek a tunnel into the earth or a stairway into the sky to bring them a sign, [then do so]. But if Allah had willed, He would have united them upon guidance. So never be of the ignorant.﴿

64. Surah An ʿām 6:52

﴿وَلَا تَطْرُدِ الَّذِينَ يَدْعُونَ رَبَّهُم بِالْغَدَاةِ وَالْعَشِيِّ يُرِيدُونَ وَجْهَهُ ۖ مَا عَلَيْكَ مِنْ حِسَابِهِم مِّن
شَيْءٍ وَمَا مِنْ حِسَابِكَ عَلَيْهِم مِّن شَيْءٍ فَتَطْرُدَهُمْ فَتَكُونَ مِنَ الظَّالِمِينَ﴾

﴾And do not send away those who call upon their Lord morning and afternoon, seeking His countenance. Not upon you is anything of their account and not upon them is anything of your account. So were you to send them away, you would then be of the wrongdoers.﴿

65. Surah Fatḥ 48:1-2

﴿إِنَّا فَتَحْنَا لَكَ فَتْحًا مُّبِينًا ﴿١﴾ لِّيَغْفِرَ لَكَ اللَّهُ مَا تَقَدَّمَ مِن ذَنبِكَ وَمَا تَأَخَّرَ وَيُتِمَّ نِعْمَتَهُ عَلَيْكَ وَيَهْدِيَكَ صِرَاطًا مُّسْتَقِيمًا﴾

﴿Indeed, We have given you, [O Muhammad], a clear conquest﴾ ﴿That Allah may forgive for you what preceded of your sin and what will follow and complete His favour upon you and guide you to a straight path.﴾

66. Surah Aḥzāb 33:37

﴿وَإِذْ تَقُولُ لِلَّذِي أَنْعَمَ اللَّهُ عَلَيْهِ وَأَنْعَمْتَ عَلَيْهِ أَمْسِكْ عَلَيْكَ زَوْجَكَ وَاتَّقِ اللَّهَ وَتُخْفِي فِي نَفْسِكَ مَا اللَّهُ مُبْدِيهِ وَتَخْشَى النَّاسَ وَاللَّهُ أَحَقُّ أَن تَخْشَاهُ ۖ فَلَمَّا قَضَىٰ زَيْدٌ مِّنْهَا وَطَرًا زَوَّجْنَاكَهَا لِكَيْ لَا يَكُونَ عَلَى الْمُؤْمِنِينَ حَرَجٌ فِي أَزْوَاجِ أَدْعِيَائِهِمْ إِذَا قَضَوْا مِنْهُنَّ وَطَرًا ۚ وَكَانَ أَمْرُ اللَّهِ مَفْعُولًا﴾

﴿And [remember, O Muhammad], when you said to the one on whom Allah bestowed favour and you bestowed favour, "Keep your wife and fear Allah ," while you concealed within yourself that which Allah is to disclose. And you feared the people, while Allah has more right that you fear Him. So when Zayd had no longer any need for her, We married her to you in order that there not be upon the believers any discomfort concerning the wives of their adopted sons when they no longer have need of them. And ever is the command of Allah accomplished.﴾

67. Surah Yūnus 10:88

﴿ رَبَّنَا اطْمِسْ عَلَىٰ أَمْوَالِهِمْ وَاشْدُدْ عَلَىٰ قُلُوبِهِمْ فَلَا يُؤْمِنُوا حَتَّىٰ يَرَوُا الْعَذَابَ الْأَلِيمَ﴾

﴿Our Lord, obliterate their wealth and harden their hearts so that they will not believe until they see the painful punishment.﴾

68. Surah Anfāl 8:68

﴿لَّوْلَا كِتَابٌ مِّنَ اللَّهِ سَبَقَ لَمَسَّكُمْ فِيمَا أَخَذْتُمْ عَذَابٌ عَظِيمٌ﴾

﴿If not for a decree from Allah that preceded, you would have been touched for what you took by a great punishment﴾

69. Surah Fatḥ 48:2

﴿مَا تَقَدَّمَ مِن ذَنبِكَ وَمَا تَأَخَّرَ﴾

﴾...what preceded of your sins and what will follow...﴿

70. Surah Aḥzāb 33:37

﴿وَإِذْ تَقُولُ لِلَّذِي أَنْعَمَ اللَّهُ عَلَيْهِ وَأَنْعَمْتَ عَلَيْهِ أَمْسِكْ عَلَيْكَ زَوْجَكَ وَاتَّقِ اللَّهَ وَتُخْفِي فِي
نَفْسِكَ مَا اللَّهُ مُبْدِيهِ وَتَخْشَى النَّاسَ وَاللَّهُ أَحَقُّ أَن تَخْشَاهُ﴾

﴾And [remember, O Muhammad], when you said to the one on whom Allah bestowed favor and you bestowed favor, "Keep your wife and fear Allah," while you concealed within yourself that which Allah is to disclose. And you feared the people, while Allah has more right that you fear Him.﴿

71. Surah Aḥzāb 33:36

﴿وَمَا كَانَ لِمُؤْمِنٍ وَلَا مُؤْمِنَةٍ إِذَا قَضَى اللَّهُ وَرَسُولُهُ أَمْرًا أَن يَكُونَ لَهُمُ الْخِيَرَةُ مِنْ أَمْرِهِمْ﴾

﴾It is not for a believing man or a believing woman, when Allah and His Messenger have decided a matter, that they should thereafter have any choice about their affair.﴿

72. Surah Aḥzāb 33:37

﴿لِكَيْ لَا يَكُونَ عَلَى الْمُؤْمِنِينَ حَرَجٌ فِي أَزْوَاجِ أَدْعِيَائِهِمْ إِذَا قَضَوْا مِنْهُنَّ وَطَرًا ۚ
وَكَانَ أَمْرُ اللَّهِ مَفْعُولًا﴾

﴾...in order that there not be upon the believers any discomfort concerning the wives of their adopted sons when they no longer have need of them. And ever is the command of Allah accomplished.﴿

73. Surah Aḥzāb 33:37

﴿فَلَمَّا قَضَىٰ زَيْدٌ مِّنْهَا وَطَرًا زَوَّجْنَاكَهَا﴾

﴾So when Zayd had no longer any need for her, We married her to you...﴿

Index of Hadiths

Hadith 1

"Whoever amongst you is put to trial with the least of these spiritual diseases should conceal it because whoever exposes it to us, then we will establish the decree of Allah" or similar to that has been transmitted. Meaning, whoever exposes his disobedience and announces it must have the legal Islamic punishment applied upon him."

According to my knowledge – the Messenger of Allah ﷺ spoke about how Allah protected him in his childhood in the Age of Ignorance when he ﷺ said:

Hadith 2

"You would have seen me among the young boys of Quraysh; we were moving stones and would play the way boys would play with them while all of us were uncovered. We would put our wraparound (izār) on our shoulders to carry the stones on it, and I would go and come with them. When suddenly someone punched me with a painful blow then said: 'Tie your izār properly!' Accordingly I took it and tied it on myself properly among my friends."

والذي نفسي بيده ما رآك الشيطان سالكا فجا إلا سلك فجا غير فجك يا عمر

Hadith 3

"I swear by the One in whose hand is my soul, Satan does not see you taking one pathway save he will take another path other than your path, O ʿUmar."

Hadith 4

"Ibrahim ﷺ did not lie except three 'lies': two of them between him and his people, his word ﴿إني سقيم﴾ or ﴿Indeed, I am sick﴾[1] and his word ﴿بل فعله كبيرهم هذا﴾ or ﴿Rather, the biggest of them did it﴾,[2] and the Prophet ﵇ said, " One day, he and Sarah came upon a tyrant [Nimrod] from among tyrants. It was said to [the tyrant]: Certainly, there is a man and a woman from the best of people.' Then the tyrant sent someone to Ibrahim ﵇ and asked about her: 'Who is she?' He said: 'my sister.'"

Ibrahim ﵇ went and said to her: 'Truly, if this tyrant comes to know you are my wife, he will overpower me and take you. So if he asks you, then tell him you are my sister....because you are my sister in Islam and there are no believers on the face of the earth other than me and you.'

The tyrant then sends for her and she was brought. Then Ibrahim ﵇ stood up and began praying ṣalah. And when she came to the tyrant, he went to grab her with his hand. Suddenly, he became paralyzed until his feet began to tremble. He said: 'Pray to Allah for me and I will not hurt you.' Accordingly she prayed to Allah and he released her. Then, he tried to grab her a second time, but was seized like before or more severe. He said: 'Pray to Allah for me and I will not hurt you. She prayed to Allah and he decided to release her from his custody. He summoned some of his chamberlains and said: 'You did not bring me a human, you only brought me a devil!' Consequently Hājar was given to provide services for Sārah. She [Sārah] came to Ibrahim ﵇ while he was standing and performing ṣalah and he gestured with his hand. She said: "Allah has repulsed the plot of the disbeliever back down his throat. So I was given Hājar to provide services.' Abu Hurairah ؓ said: "That is your mother, O Arabs (lit. O children of water from the sky)." (Bukhārī and Muslim)

Hadith 5

"Verily Allah has recorded the good deeds and the evil deeds." Then he clarified that: "Whosoever intends to do a good deed but does not do it, Allah records it with Himself as a complete good deed; but if he intends it and does it, Allah records it with Himself as ten good deeds, up to seven hundred times, or more than that. But if he intends to do an evil deed and does not do it, Allah records it with Himself as a complete

---

1 Quran 37:89 (Saffat)

2 Quran 21:63 (Anbiya')

good deed; but if he intends it and does it, Allah records it down as one single evil deed."(Bukhari & Muslim)

Hadith 6

Tirmidhi, Ḥākim and Bayhaqī narrate that Ibn Mas'ūd رضي الله عنه said,

"On the day of Badr, captives were brought.[3]

Abu Bakr رضي الله عنه said, 'O Messenger of Allah, they are your people, your family. Release them, perhaps Allah will forgive them.'

'Umar رضي الله عنه said, 'O Messenger of Allah, they belied you, they exiled you, and they fought against you. Put them forward and execute them.'

'Abdullah ibn Rawāḥah رضي الله عنه said, 'Look for a valley with plenty of dried wood and burn them in a fire.'

As a result 'Abbās رضي الله عنه said while hearing what they were saying, '[Were you to do so,] you will sever your family ties.'

So the Prophet ﷺ retreated to his tent and he did not respond to them whatsoever. Some people said: 'he agrees with the opinion of Abu Bakr رضي الله عنه'. Still some said 'he agrees with the opinion of 'Umar رضي الله عنه'. Then the Messenger of Allah ﷺ exited and said,

(إن الله ليلين قلوب رجال حتى تكون ألين من اللبن. وإن الله ليشدد قلوب رجال حتى تكون أشد من الحجارة)

"Truly, Allah will soften the hearts of men until they become softer than yogurt. Indeed, Allah will hardens the hearts of men until they become harder than stone."

Your example, O Abu Bakr, is like that of Ibrāhīm عليه السلام when He said,

﴿فمن تبعني فإنه مني، ومن عصاني فإنك غفور رحيم﴾

Or

﴿...so whoever follows me - then he is of me; and whoever disobeys me - indeed, You are yet Forgiving and Merciful.﴾ [Surah Ibrāhīm 14:36]

Your example, O Abu Bakr, is like that of 'Īsā عليه السلام when he said,

---

[3] i.e. hostile enemies of the state – trans.

﴿إِن تُعَذِّبْهُمْ فَإِنَّهُمْ عِبَادُكَ ۖ وَإِن تَغْفِرْ لَهُمْ فَإِنَّكَ أَنتَ الْعَزِيزُ الْحَكِيمُ﴾ or ﴿If You should punish them - indeed they are Your servants; but if You forgive them - indeed it is You who is the Exalted in Might, the Wise﴾ [Surah Mā'ida 5:118]

And your example, O 'Umar, is like that of Nūḥ ﷺ when he said,

﴿رَّبِّ لَا تَذَرْ عَلَى الْأَرْضِ مِنَ الْكَافِرِينَ دَيَّارًا﴾ or ﴿My Lord, do not leave upon the earth from among the disbelievers an inhabitant﴾ [Surah Nūḥ 71:26]

And your example, O 'Umar, is like that of Mūsā ﷺ when he said,

﴿رَبَّنَا اطْمِسْ عَلَىٰ أَمْوَالِهِمْ وَاشْدُدْ عَلَىٰ قُلُوبِهِمْ فَلَا يُؤْمِنُوا حَتَّىٰ يَرَوُا الْعَذَابَ الْأَلِيمَ﴾ or ﴿Our Lord, obliterate their wealth and harden their hearts so that they will not believe until they see the painful punishment﴾ [Surah Yūnus 10:88]

Then he ﷺ said, "All of you are related to us, so none of you will be released except by ransom or execution."

Subsequently 'Abdullah said: "O Messenger of Allah, except Suhayl ibn Bayḍā' because I heard him mentioning Islam.[4] So Allah's Messenger ﷺ became silent. You have never seen me on any day anyone more frightened that stones were going to be pelted at me than that day until Allah's Messenger ﷺ said, "Except Suhayl ibn Bayḍā." Then Allah Most High revealed the verse:

﴿مَا كَانَ لِنَبِيٍّ أَن يَكُونَ لَهُ أَسْرَىٰ حَتَّىٰ يُثْخِنَ فِي الْأَرْضِ...﴾

﴿It is not for a prophet to have captives of war until he inflicts a massacre [upon Allah 's enemies] in the land...﴾

[Surah Anfāl 8:67]

Hadith 7

It is narrated by Aḥmad and Muslim from the ḥadīth of Ibn 'Abbās ؓ, "When the captives were captured, referring to the Day of Badr, Allah's Messenger ﷺ said to Abu Bakr ؓ and 'Umar ؓ, 'what do you think we should do with these captives?' Abu Bakr ؓ said, 'O Messenger of Allah, they are our cousins and our close relatives, we think you should take a

4 i.e. He was talking about embracing Islam - trans

ransom for them, it will be leverage for us against the disbelievers. Perhaps Allah will guide them to Islam.' Allah's Messenger ﷺ said, 'What do you think, O son of Khaṭṭāb?'

He replied, 'No, I swear by Allah, O Messenger of Allah, I don't see it the same way Abu Bakr does. Rather, I think we should seize the opportunity, take control and execute them. 'Alī should take Aqīl [his brother] and execute him, and I should take so-and-so and execute him ['Umar's relative], and so-and-so should take so-and-so his relative because they are the leaders of disbelief and their advocates.'

'Thereafter the Messenger of Allah ﷺ inclined towards what Abu Bakr ؓ said and he did not incline to what I said. So when the morrow came, I approached and noticed the Messenger of Allah ﷺ and Abu Bakr sitting and weeping. I said, 'O Messenger of Allah, inform me what is making you cry and your companion,[5] so if I can cry, I will. And if I cannot cry, I will make myself cry because both of you are crying! The Messenger of Allah ﷺ said: "Cry over what your companion [referring to himself] opined about accepting ransom for them. It has been shown to me that their punishment should be closer than this tree (a tree that was very close to him). Then Allah revealed the verse:

﴿ مَا كَانَ لِنَبِيٍّ أَن يَكُونَ لَهُ أَسْرَىٰ حَتَّىٰ يُثْخِنَ فِي الْأَرْضِ... ﴾

﴾It is not for a prophet to have captives of war until he inflicts a massacre [upon Allah 's enemies] in the land...﴿

[Surah Anfāl 8:87]

"We have more propensity to doubt than Ibrahim ؑ."

Hadith 8

"Indeed, the noble one (al-karīm), the son of the noble one, the son of the noble one; Yusūf the son of Yaqūb, the son of Isḥāq, the son of Ibrāhīm.

﴿إن الكريم بن الكريم بن الكريم، يوسف بن يعقوب، بن اسحق، بن إبراهيم﴾

[5] 'Your companion' here refers to Abu Bakr ؓ - trans